first aid

aid

F O R

the betrayed

recovering from the devastation of an affair;
A PERSONAL GUIDE TO HEALING

by

RICHARD ALAN

Trafford
PUBLISHING®

www.trafford.com

North America & international
toll-free: 1 888 232 4444 (USA & Canada)
phone: 250 383 6864 ♦ fax: 250 383 6804
email: info@trafford.com

The United Kingdom & Europe
phone: +44 (0)1865 722 113 ♦ local rate: 0845 230 9601
facsimile: +44 (0)1865 722 868 ♦ email: info.uk@trafford.com

10 9 8 7 6 5 4 3

Preface to the Expanded Edition

In the two years since I wrote the first printing of this book much has happened in my life and I've continued to learn more from people like you who have been so painfully betrayed. I've received many reader questions as to the state of my own recovery and that of my marriage. The good news is that I've finally found equilibrium in my life and our marriage is much better than it was four years ago when my wife's infidelity was first discovered. I offer that mainly to assure you that life can become normal and you can find happiness again.

Infidelity continues to be a major relationship problem and though the marriage and relationship improvement industry has not been able to stop it, we at least have learned more about it and ways to recover. I've also found that there is a dearth of help for those who commit adultery who genuinely want to atone for their actions and repair the damage. Though this book remains a primary "first aid manual" for the betrayed partner, I've added a section that addresses the betrayer and offers advice to the one who is serious about making up for their betrayal.

This expanded edition adds new material and broadens some of the old to further help you in recovering from the devastation that has descended upon you. As always, my prayers, hopes and best wishes go out to you for a swift recovery and a future full of happiness and love.

Richard Alan, June, 2008

Dedication

This book is dedicated to you, all those who have gone before you and those who will follow, that have suffered the ultimate indignity and devastation of a loved one's betrayal of trust by infidelity. It is especially dedicated to Peggy Vaughan and the coordinators and members of the Beyond Affairs Network (beyondaffairs.com). Special thanks to those in my own BAN support group particularly those who helped establish the group; Dan, Susan, Natalie, Pam, Kimberly and Ivy. Dr. D., my caring and compassionate counselor deserves special credit for saving my life. My heart has been healed thanks to all of you. I'd like to acknowledge the support of all the members of our support group for their inspiration and ideas that have helped formulate my thoughts for this book

Finally, I'd like to devote this book to my wife who has tried mightily to make up for her betrayal of our marriage. Before the affair, she was always my guiding light, a woman of accomplishment who I respected, loved and adored. Through this journey, she has once again proved that her strength of character can overcome great difficulties. My greatest hope is that she will find peace in her soul and once again become the woman of my dreams.

Contents:

Forward

The state of marriage and committed relationships in the world, especially in America has become an issue of great importance over the last few years. Politicians have staked out their positions on issues such as homosexual marriage and the lines have been drawn. Many say that the very institution of marriage is under attack. I have to say that seems to be very much to be the case. But, in a way, it always has been. In her groundbreaking book, *The Monogamy Myth*, Peggy Vaughan clearly exposes the ill founded belief that marriage means monogamy and togetherness forever. In fact, we now know that up half and by some estimates, more marriages involve infidelity.

Adultery and deception in relationships have been with us since the dawn of time. Great men and women across the sands of time have shown their duplicity through dalliances and intensely sexual affairs. The tales of sin and adultery are exposed in the bible and other religious tracts. In God's own commandments, adultery stands beside murder and theft as a most serious violation of law and acceptable behavior. For centuries, affairs were seen to be the province of men only and women seemed to be left to suffer in silent acceptance since it was often seen as a case of "boys will be boys." One has to wonder though, who were these men having their affairs with? Certainly not always other men so the role of women may not have been such a silent suffering at all but more a silent hidden role that only in the last few years has exploded to the point where women now have reached parity with men in their participation in affairs and the deceit that goes with them.

Our society used to condemn such activities and those who participated were scourged and publicly humiliated. Today, we celebrate it through films, books, television programs that give reason to believe that adultery is fun, exciting and even justified. Movies such as *The Bridges of Madison County* and television shows such as *Desperate Housewives* show just how pervasive our permissiveness and acceptance of this behavior is today. It is as though while 50% of the married people are having affairs, the other 50% are enjoying it by proxy. Some advertisers even stoop to using adultery or illicit activities as an enticement to buy their products. The most blatant such advertising were the automobile billboards and advertisements by General Motors in 2005 that encouraged male buyers to buy two cars, one for the wife and one for the mistress.

The steamy sexual energy generated by affairs is akin to drugs. In fact, the release of all those hormonal cocktails is intoxicating and causes such a high for most adulterers that it is almost as addictive as cocaine. In many respects, we are waging a war on adultery that is as abject a failure as the war on drugs. An entire industry has flourished that addresses prevention of affairs, recovery from affairs, improving marriages and male – female relationships. Despite that, the incidence of adultery continues to skyrocket to the point where more than half of us are in some way involved and it the other half is suffering the devastating effects of their actions.

Just as drugs ruin lives and families, so too does adultery. Somewhere in the romance and glorification of affairs, we have never noticed the terrible damage it does to the lives of many people. Where a drug addict ruins relationships, causes financial damage and hurts innocents, so too do affairs. If you are reading this as one who has been hurt (an understatement for those who have experienced it) you know exactly what I mean. Affairs suck the life out of marriages and individuals. Just as drug addicts do, adulterers spend outrageous amounts of money on their habit. They shower their lovers with gifts, entertainment and spend thousands on travel and hotels while family bills go unpaid. Affairs remove one parent almost entirely from the free time of families. They are so driven to get their high that they will find ways to spend every free moment to be with their paramour rather than their mates and children. The intoxication of an affair can cause otherwise rational people to act irrationally.

In their excitement, the errant spouses often believe they are smarter than everyone else. They often believe that they can live two lives, maintain their lover and avoid detection. They can't and don't. They always get caught, always, because in their euphoria, they often become very foolish. Those of us who are betrayed can feel the change in them, we know something is up and soon discover the infidelity through simple investigation. They always leave a trail. And in the end, there is destruction.

Though the destruction and cost of drug addiction has been publicized and used to discourage it, the destruction caused by an affair has been largely ignored in favor of the glory and profit potential of either exposing the sordid details or exploiting it through forms of entertainment that are questionable at best. Springer, Maury and their breed exploit the pain and anguish of those who have been betrayed shamelessly and incessantly. Yet we watch. If you've ever watched the angry reactions of those who discover an affair on those shows and believe it is all a scripted reaction, think again. That kind of reaction is real and it is common.

Those who have been betrayed suffer pain and emotional destruction that goes beyond description. The children of parents whose marriage is destroyed suffer emotional scars that last a lifetime and often drive them into similar behavior when they become adults. Mothers, fathers, sisters, brothers and friends are severely distressed and angered by affairs. Some would disagree but I believe that no good, none, ever comes out of an affair and once it is done and in the open, we are left to pick up the pieces and rebuild our lives.

Recovery and rebuilding your life after an affair is in the opinion of those who have been so betrayed, the most difficult challenge that a person can face in life. Most agree that even the death of your closest loved one is easier to accept and recover from. Death can be understood and is expected. Betrayal by the one person you love the most and in whose care you have entrusted your heart is overwhelming, unexpected and incomprehensible. In dealing with over one hundred victims of affairs, every one of them has said it is the worst experience of their life. One cancer survivor said that hearing she had cancer was less an emotional blow than discovering her husband's affair! It is almost impossible to accept and can never be forgotten. It can however, be overcome.

Why people have affairs is complex. Not everyone who has an affair is an evil selfish harmful person. Good people fall into affairs never intending to do harm. Unfortunately, some are evil and some do it as a hobby without regard for the consequences to others. This book cannot even begin to analyze the why and how of affairs. For the best understanding of that, read the aforementioned *Monogamy Myth*.

This book is about hope, healing and knowing that the hell you are going through as a betrayed partner can be overcome. It is about finding your way out of the fog of emotional and physical destruction that you are feeling. It is about shedding the fear, anger and humiliation and rebuilding your self esteem and happiness. So many others have faced this challenge over the centuries and almost all of them have found a new life and overcome the destruction. You will too.

Once, at a conference of Christian counselors I expressed my view that the attempts to prevent affairs were a losing battle, just like the war on drugs seems to be. I asked aloud, "why bother, it seems the marriage building industry is a very ineffective one for the incidence of infidelity continues to rise. While self-help and marriage help has grown, so too has adultery." An elevator companion who overheard my comments simply said, "We don't give up the war on drugs because it is the right thing to do and if we did, it would only be worse. It's the same with the war on infidelity; we can't give up and if we save just one marriage or prevent just one affair, it is all worth it."

Regrettably, for most readers, this book means we failed you personally. But hopefully, we can help you heal and from this terrible ordeal, build a better life and a better future relationship. God bless you and good luck in your healing.

Note:

In most cases, infidelity takes place in a marriage setting. As such, much of what I say relates to marriages but I fully understand that any committed relationship can and often does involve infidelity and the pain and devastation is no less for you than a married person. For convenience, I have mostly used the term "partner" to refer to the person in your life who betrayed your trust. I am well aware that the pain of betrayal of trust is no less for those whose spouse, fiancé, life partner or other committed person has betrayed you.

Caution:

This book contains actual dialogues or journal entries that I wrote during the discovery and aftermath of my wife's affair. Some of these passages are extremely graphic at times and contain very harsh language and sexual content. If you are going through the aftermath of an affair, you will understand. I apologize for any offensive passages but feel that the truth must be told and hope that by seeing these passages the reader will gain an understanding of the difficult consequences of marital infidelity and see that they are not alone in their intense emotions and reactions.

THE CURSE OF AN ACHING HEART

You made me think you cared for me,
And I believed in you.
You told me things you never meant,
And made me think them true.
I gambled in the game of love,
I played my heart and lost.
I'm now a wreck, Upon life's sea,
Alone I pay the cost.

You made me what I am today,
I hope you're satisfied,
You dragged and dragged me down until
My soul within me died;
You've shattered each and ev'ry dream,
You fooled me from the start,
And though you're not true,
May God bless you,
That's the curse of an aching heart.

The dreams I dreamed of future joys,
You smiled on, though you knew,
Deep down within your faithless heart,
They never would come true,
Still further on you lead me
till my paradise I saw,
Then with one word you banished
all my hopes for ever more.

You made me what I am today,
I hope you're satisfied,
You dragged and dragged me down until
My soul within me died;

You've shattered each and ev'ry dream,
You fooled me from the start,
And though you're not true,
May God bless you,
That's the curse of an aching heart.

Original Lyrics from a song with music by AL.
PIANTADOSI and words by HENRY FINK. Published
1913 by LEO. FEIST, Inc.

Getting Started

The Ultimate Betrayal

I remember my wedding day so clearly. My wife to be was my dream come true and I just knew she was my soul mate. We were so loving and caring about each other and we just knew that we would always be in love and together till death. We stood before God, our families, our friends, the attendants and the pastor and vowed that we would love, honor and keep one another to the exclusion of all others. We talked of miracles like our marriage, having children and growing old together. We even talked of how we would never cheat on each other and if we did there would be hell to pay.

Like all couples that marry, we believed that our love would always carry us through the hard times and we would be true to one another forever. We placed our hearts in each other's hands for safekeeping and trusted each other to always be honest and caring. Just like you and your partner or special person undoubtedly did.

The marriage vows are, without question, a couple's most emotionally binding act of faith and trust. The coming together of two people in marriage (or a committed relationship) creates a special bond that is unlike any other contract between two people on this earth. It is a bond forged in love and welded together by trust. Our very life's security from that time forward is founded on our marriage vows and commitment to each other. When we marry, we truly do merge our hearts, lives and souls.

Marriage is a stronger bond for many than that to parents, siblings and every other person on earth. Though we love our families, we did not choose them. We were born into that family and were nurtured and loved from the beginning, which in turn engendered our own love for the family. But, familial love is a sort of love that is far different from the romantic love of choice we make for ourselves with a partner. Through falling in love and building a mutual bond of choice, we find ourselves in a relationship that is truly made in heaven and with the strongest emotional bindings that a man and woman can create for each other.

When that bond, those vows and that trust is broken by one partner's willful decision to engage in a secret emotional or sexual affair with another, the betrayal becomes the most painful and devastating human experience of all. And with that devastation comes one of the most difficult and longest roads to recovery to regain your self-esteem, trust, health and mental equilibrium. You must deal with emotional pain that is as physical as any knife wound, a loss of self and so many other issues that it seems impossible that we will be able to live and love ever again.

Unfortunately, if you have a need to read this book, my heart goes out to you. You've joined a club that no one wants to be a member of and none of us ever thought we'd be a part of. If a partner has betrayed you, this book will help guide you towards a new life (with or without your partner) and help you to heal and enjoy life again. It will not erase the painful memories that you have; those will always be with you but it will help you heal the destruction wrought upon you by your unfaithful partner.

What This Book Is About.

In a word, healing; personally healing the damage done to you as a result of your partner's betrayal. It may help to say what the book is *not* about or to compare it to other books about affairs. It is not so much about intellectual understanding of affairs, rebuilding a marriage, research into affairs and their childhood or other causes as it is about giving you help to get past the darkest days of emotional pain after discovery of a partner's affair. Though I may mention those issues and provide some information related to them in order to ensure that there is a general understanding or to provide background for some of the ideas, suggested activities and discussions in the book, it is not intended to be an in depth examination of those issues.

There are many excellent books on those subjects and a list of recommended books appears in Chapter 19. I suggest you read one or two of those books while working through this one or soon after so that you'll have the larger view of the issue. Many such books help provide the understanding needed as a foundation for healing. I've also found that reading and learning about affairs, relationships and recovery is therapeutic as well. By reading, your mind is diverted from the emotional level to a more objective and intellectual understanding of your situation

This book is also not a replacement for personal counseling by a professional. Many, if not all of us who've experienced an affair have sought counseling and psychiatric help. There is no shame in that. In my own case I was so depressed and suicidal I believe that if I had not reached out for help, someone else would be writing this, or no one would. *If you are having serious thoughts of suicide or depression that are interfering with your ability to function normally, put this book down right now and call a local clinic or suicide help line for help.* Once you are in their care and ready, pick up this book again.

Through this book, I hope to help you look at what happened to you more objectively than you may be able to do now depending on how long it has been since the day you discovered the infidelity. I also hope to help you identify the issues that are most troubling you. I'll provide you with insights from some of those who have gone before you and give you practical ideas for dealing with the myriad of emotions, concerns, problems and agonies of being betrayed by someone you love. In some ways this book is a first aid guide that allows you to build your own future. It will, I hope, allow you to be the architect of your own healing and get you moving in a positive direction that will ultimately allow you to push the pain aside and resume a "normal" life and meaningful, trusting relationships.

This book is not intended to be your sole source for recovery. Though my desire is to give you hope and help for the future, you'll need other means of support. Your partner can play an important part in your recovery but may not cooperate. You'll need the support and understanding of friends and family. I strongly urge you to seek out a support group that will give you the strength and understanding needed to overcome your grief. The only such national network is the Beyond Affairs Network (BAN) organized by the foremost authority on affairs, Peggy Vaughan. I'll have much more to say about Peggy and BAN later. Visit the Beyond Affairs website web site at beyondaffairs.com to learn about the network she founded and to find one of the support groups near you. Her dearpeggy.com site is also the best resource on the net for information about affairs and healing.

How to Use This Book

This is not a book to educate you as much as it is a guide to simply help you pull yourself out of the emotional hell you find yourself in today. As such, you need not read it in order, you need not read it all or, I suppose you don't really have to read any of it. However, that would certainly be a waste of the price paid! It's your choice. The book deals with the major issues that we all must overcome in order to heal and offers you some ideas and examples that are designed to get you moving in the right direction to recovery.

You can simply thumb through the book and go directly to the issue that is troubling you the most and deal with it first. Then you can approach the other subjects based on where you are feeling the most pain or need. If some of the issues are not of concern to you, you can save yourself some time and bypass them. If they later become an issue you can come back to the book at that time. Otherwise, you can just put the book in a drawer or bookcase and be done with it. At some point, I truly hope you never need this book again and you can perhaps pass it on to someone else in need.

In some sections, there are simple questions you can ask yourself to help explore your own feelings and needs and then there are some simple and effective ways to help you cope and get past the obstacles to healing. The ideas and suggestions come from many sources including people just like you and I who have faced this betrayal. It's not a bunch of psychological mumbo-jumbo. It is reality, what you feel, and how you can cope with it and overcome the devastation you face.

Devastation; Your World Crumbles

Discovery and the end of your world

Most of us who have discovered the truth about a partner's affair call the date when we finally got the evidence, or they confessed, our "D" (discovery) day. Mine was fittingly, April Fools Day 2004. That day is etched into my mind as the most traumatic and painful day of my life. I can still remember the first feelings of despair while my heart almost stopped beating. Within moments, I felt devastated, destroyed. My world crumbled in a moment and it seemed as though everything I thought to be true about my marriage and my life was nothing more than an illusion. In that same instant, I lost my own identity as well as the identity of my wife. Who was this woman? Certainly not the woman I thought she was. Neither was she the woman I married. It's as though an evil spirit, a demon, had been hiding beneath the shell of the woman I thought loved me and then revealed her self as the fiend from hell she seemed to really be.

A split second later I fell into the deepest despair I've ever felt before and never felt since. The emotional pain in my heart became physical. A mental anguish that was as painful as the worst physical torture one could imagine. Soon after this came the anger; a seething almost homicidal anger that was directed at her and the lover she took behind my back and kept for months while living a lie with me. I wanted to hurt someone, anyone and felt as though if the lover appeared at that moment, I am sure I would have killed him in a fit of rage.

All this was the equivalent of a nuclear device exploding within my brain, totally annihilating every thing dear to me and literally tearing the joy of life out of me. Finally, I turned on myself. What a fool I had been, what an idiot. A worthless piece of garbage that could not even keep his wife satisfied. I felt unattractive, worthless, sexually inadequate and rejected in a way that seemed unimaginable. I begged God to take me out of my pain. I wanted to die. I even held a loaded gun to my head. I was destroyed in the flash of an instant. I was changed forever, my wife was someone different, never again to be the person I married and my marriage was crushed into dust.

One of the most often repeated reactions to discovery of an affair is the feeling that the world you thought you lived in was all a lie. At the same time, you have probably asked yourself; "who is this person I am married to?" Almost every one of us who have faced this situation realizes that our partner seems to no longer be the person we fell in love with. All that we thought they were is gone in an instant, replaced by a stranger we do not know or understand. Along with these feelings we suddenly find ourselves desperately insecure. The safety of our world has dissolved in a matter of moments and we feel so unsafe, alone and afraid. One of the people in my support group had this to say about the transformation:

> "She has turned into an alien being. She really has gone crazy. We had a good marriage and I was the doting husband, caring and loving father to our children. We were in church every Sunday, I taught Sunday school, she taught children's choir, sang in the choir and women of praise. It makes no sense. It is almost as if she snapped

somehow and became a different person overnight. I will never figure it out and thankfully for the most part have quit trying. Everything and everyone that was once sacred to her and important to her mean nothing, including family, children, friends, church, standards, morals, etc. She has a whole new life consisting of this other man."

I think my story of discovery and the reaction I had is probably very much like your own. Though the circumstances may be different, every person who has been similarly betrayed has experienced the same emotions. You are not alone in your devastation. We all search for words strong enough to truly describe the event and we all seem to come up short. Devastation is the best word anyone has been able to find that even comes close. You entire world is wiped out in a moment as though a cataclysmic nuclear event had vaporized everything you know. You stand in a wasteland devoid of safety, security and comfort.

I know in my heart that you have felt these same things and possibly much more. I personally believe that the betrayal of a partner is worse than the death of your closest relative or even that partner. You can understand the reasons a loved one dies, yes it hurts but they did not intentionally leave you (except in cases of suicide) and you can comprehend the loss. An affair by someone you trusted is not at all easy to understand and you'll agonize for weeks, months even years searching for the reasons why. A death has a finality that can be placed behind you relatively quickly and the pain is replaced most often by fond memories of good times together. In the case of an affair, the offender is still before you, often in your life and a constant reminder of what they did. Sometimes they make your life hell by taunting you and driving the pain ever deeper. In many cases, when children are involved, the person stays closely tied to you and even in cases where divorce results from the affair, you are unable to purge them from your life.

Those of us who have been through what you are going through may be the only ones who truly understand the depth of pain you are feeling. Without question, I believe the betrayal of an affair to be the single most devastating life event that you'll ever face.

You'll be off balance for a long time and some days it will seem impossible to get up or function. You'll hate your job and sometimes be afraid to go to work or be away from your partner for fear that they will immediately call their lover and find comfort in their arms.

Within a couple of days of discovery of my wife's affair, I started a journal to document my feelings and what was happening. I did it mainly because I needed an outlet for my feelings. I'll say more about journaling later (do it!) but to illustrate the feelings on discovery, I'll share some of the early entries. These have been edited very little and my emotions and anger were very raw, however I've left a lot of the rawness in so you can see that you are not alone in how you feel; we all go through this.

> "My world ended today. April fucking fools! After years of tensions in our marriage, I discovered that (my wife) was having an affair with another man. I felt it all along, just did not have proof till now. She had left a years worth of e-mail to him in her outbox describing in graphic detail how they fucked and how she wanted to spread her legs for him. I went ballistic, screaming, crying and yelling and getting in her face. My first response was to kill the son of a bitch. I grabbed my gun and left the house to find him and blow his dick off."

I went on describing my reactions:

> "I can't begin to describe the feelings I had. I was desperate and felt completely deceived and abandoned. The woman whom I had loved for over twenty years had lied to me for years, had ruined our financial lives and put our marriage in jeopardy had finally committed the ultimate act of betrayal. She had given that which should only have been mine to an asshole that played her like a fiddle and just wanted another piece of ass. I hate her and at the same time love her. My heart is broken and my life seems ended. I want to die and find peace and escape from her betrayal. I took off towards Birmingham, driving and crying and praying to God for help. Half the time I could not see through the tears."

It may be that you were not so violently affected, I hope not. If you were or are now, take comfort, it will get better. Ok, you ask, how could it be any worse? It's important to me that you see that you are not alone in your pain. Yes, your situation is unique in its facts and circumstances but the devastation and feelings of blame, inadequacy, fear, aloneness and confusion is something we've all felt. You are not going crazy and you are not the reason this happened.

It's Not YOUR Fault

Right now we need to start you off in the right direction. Say this out loud: It's not MY fault. Say it over an over for there is no other absolute truth for you that will come out of this situation. By now, it's even possible that your partner has already given you a hundred reasons why they believe it *is* your fault. Don't let them convince you that it is. Keep some important points in mind:

- They are the one who made the conscious choice to have an affair. They had many more choices, certainly better ones than lying to you, having sex with someone behind your back or sharing intimate thoughts with someone else. They could have told you the truth, they could have divorced you or left you first, they could have had the common courtesy and compassion to simply tell you they were ready to move on. Of all the choices they made, it seems they selected the worst for you.

- They will tell you many reasons why it is your fault: "You did not listen to me. You did not show me enough passion. You did not care about me. You were too selfish. You did not take care of yourself. You got too fat. You got too skinny. You were inconsiderate." On and on and on. Does that sound familiar?

- All of the reasons they give you are nothing but excuses and ways to avoid taking responsibility for what they have done. Do not buy any of what they are trying to sell you. I repeat; it was their choice to lie and betray; they had many other options.

- Their efforts to blame you help them deal with what must be a difficult thing to accept. In all fairness, who wants to admit that they were so uncaring about someone else whom they had vowed to love and protect? It is very difficult for some of them to admit that they committed adultery so will try every way possible to justify it by blaming you for "making" them have an affair.

It's Not About You.

Aside from it not being your fault, it is important that you realize that what he or she did was not about you. It is not a reflection of you as a person, lover, companion or person. Though they do desperately turn on you as the reason, it really has little or nothing to do with you and your value as a person. So what does it have to do with you ask?

It is all about *them*. What happened is a reflection of their own needs, desires, weaknesses and selfishness. People have affairs mostly because they are insecure, seeking a thrill, weak or pulled into a situation where they are unwilling to stop the slide into an affair. Once they begin the slippery slope into an affair, they put us out of mind and think only of themselves and self gratification. It is only later that they realize they've wronged you and that is when they begin the blame game to justify what they have done.

Most of the issues that lead someone into infidelity are almost always about them. Some people are emotionally undeveloped and in need of validation. Some people are terribly insecure, even in what most of us would consider a secure environment. Other people carry around pent up feelings that lead to vengeful actions. We used to call that "collecting brown stamps" in the training business. For those of you who are too young to remember trading stamps, they used to be issued by stores as a premium for buying from them. You collected them and traded them in for gifts and items like toasters, watches and the like. The most well known brand was S & H Green Stamps. The idea of brown stamps comes from that concept and is the opposite of a green stamp that can be cashed in for something nice.

A brown stamp collector saves up bad experiences and puts "stamps" in their mind for redemption later. So every time they think you did something wrong, they store it in their "book" rather than deal with it. Then one day they cash in all the brown stamps by doing something that hurts you. I guess it should take a lot of pent up feelings to gather enough stamps to cash in for an affair, but for some, one or two stamps might be enough to make them feel justified. These pent up feelings could so easily be dealt with in an open and honest manner but some people just can't seem to do that.

As you process what happened to you and begin to heal, you'll sometimes start to blame yourself for what happened. You'll either do that because they have told you incessantly that it is your fault, or will do it as a part of searching for understanding. You will begin to ask what you may have done that might have caused the affair. Sure, we all have our faults and we all contribute to marital or relationship strife and conflict. But get this firmly in your mind; *there is nothing you could have done that would justify them having an affair.* Oh, they will say otherwise, but think about it. What would justify YOU having an affair? I think you'll come up empty and realize that it was not you; it was their reaction and personal choice. It was all about them.

Don't begin the "what if" or "if only I'd" line of thinking. You'll get absolutely nowhere with those thoughts. There is nothing constructive about that line of thinking. For one thing, it's far too late to do anything about what happened. Punishing yourself with thoughts of what you might have been able to do before the fact to prevent it will only divert your energy and make you feel worse. It doesn't matter. In over four years of associating with and helping others like you, I've seen everything done before hand that you could think of. None of it worked for them. None of it probably would have worked for you. Those who commit adultery are the only ones who "should have" or "could have" prevented it. All they had to do was one simple thing; be honest. They chose deception and secrecy instead. Once they start down that slippery slope, there is nothing you or anyone else can do to stop it. It was entirely up to them to put on the brakes; them and only them.

Here is what one of my support group members had to say about this issue:

> "I accepted the charge that somehow I was guilty of causing the affair. My wife blamed me for letting her lover into our house. Let me explain. This man and his wife had become friends of ours and we saw them frequently on a social basis. Later she asked me if it would be alright for her to go to work for him as an electrician's helper and bookkeeper. I agreed because I knew after 9 years of marriage that my wife was not happy as a stay at home mom and never would be. This job then gave him reason to come by our house almost at will to check on job orders, etc. My wife said that if I had not agreed to let them be in such close contact with one another, the affair would not have occurred and that, therefore, I was guilty of not protecting her from a sexual predator. Since I accepted this guilt, I then had to stay and atone for what I had failed to do as a husband, i.e., protect her from this outside threat."

That is pathetic isn't it? That his wife would reach so far to blame him for her affair shows to what extent some people will go to in order to avoid accepting responsibility. Do not let this happen to you!

And, if you are still blaming yourself, read what another person in my support group said on this subject:

> "How can one partner in a marriage be responsible for what another partner decides to do when they are lying and deceitful in order to do it?

They always blame us, everything we do or don't do or don't do well enough is put on the "Reasons to Do Whatever the Hell I Please Even Though I Made a Vow to This Person" side of the ledger. Until finally they come up with the clichéd clinchers, like "I love you but I'm not in love with you" or "We never should have gotten married in the first place (See also: "We got married for the wrong reasons" and "I never loved you from the beginning") or "I've been 'unhappy' for years and years (usually accompanied by an increasing number of years on each telling)" or the time-worn "You're too old/fat/stupid/no fun/whatever they know will deflate your self-esteem fastest".

The truth is that both parties are NOT responsible unless one spouse comes to the other and says "Honey, I'm thinking about screwing that Twinkie at work and if you don't help me, you're going to end up on the business end of a divorce lawsuit." Now, if any of us heard that, and did nothing- then I'd say that we *might* be 50% responsible.

Otherwise, this whole "responsible" thing is just a way for people to protect themselves emotionally. If they can believe that we are somehow "responsible" for the fact that they can't keep their promises, then they can believe that somehow, through some magic formula, they were justified."

Those are some powerful and blunt words for you from someone else who has "been there."

Say this out loud:

> "It's not my fault that he/she chose to deceive.
> It's not my fault that he/she chose to betray.
> ### IT'S NOT MY FAULT!"

Never, *never* forget this, repeat it often and carry it in your broken heart.

Finding a New World

The Road to Recovery

You will recover. You will be able to overcome what has happened to you and regain your life and joy of life. Once we've faced the pain and begin to gain our equilibrium, we are challenged with a number of choices, all of them critical. The unfortunate part is that we are often forced into making life altering critical decisions at a time when we are least able to look at the issues objectively. As a result, I've seen a number of people make decisions about their future during the period of confusion that turn out to have been the wrong decision. Most often is the decision to immediately end the marriage.

Stan (not his real name, I've used different names to protect the possible identification of the people I quote in the book) and his wife, much like most of us, had discussed the potential of infidelity and had vowed to divorce the other if ever they discovered infidelity. I think almost all couples have that sort of discussion not really believing that it will ever happen to them. After all, when you marry you are absolutely sure that your love will last and conquer all. Your marriage will be different; special. When Stan discovered that Sally had an affair with a co-worker, without discussion he immediately told her he was making good on the promise and filed for divorce within days of discovery. Later, shortly after the divorce was finalized Stan began to have second thoughts and admitted that he really did not want to divorce Sally but felt bound by their oath. He found that he was now unable to effectively deal with many aspects of the affair and stubbornly refused to backtrack. In his words, "I promised I would divorce her and I wanted to be as true to that promise as much as our wedding vows."

It's not fair for me to say that Stan made a mistake except for his own grudging admission but his situation is a cautionary tale that should cause us to stop and think before we act. The experts tell us that some 70% (plus or minus) of all marriages where infidelity is discovered do not end in divorce, and the couple manages to learn from the situation and build a new relationship that is sometimes stronger than before. In my own dealings with over 200 individuals, the percentage is reversed; well over 70% of our people have been divorced due to infidelity. I have no proof, but based on Stan's story and others like his, I would bet that of the percentage who do divorce, a large percentage have second thoughts and later regret making the decision, especially if done in the heat of anger and the mental confusion that often comes with discovery. Don't be a stubborn chump. We all say tend to say what we would do in a given situation but when it actually happens, as you already know, it is not so clear cut.

Here is what Peggy Vaughan has to say about the odds and if you've not decided about divorce, it is well worth considering:

> "I can't provide any definitive statistics on how many married couples stay together. But I can confidently say it is more than most people assume. That's because much of time people only hear about an affair if there is a divorce - so they make the false assumption that affairs typically lead to divorce. But many/most people who stay married never tell their friends/acquaintances that this has happened.

Frank Pittman, a therapist whose clients are almost exclusively couples dealing with affairs, has said that over 70% stayed married. (Of course, as with any statistic, there are always extenuating circumstances. For instance, those couples who seek counseling are those most inclined to TRY to stay together in the first place.)

My own survey on affairs (1,083 respondents) showed that 76% stayed married. This was true whether the affair was by the husband or the wife - contrary to another common false assumption that a man will typically leave if his wife has an affair. But again, it's important to note that the people who "self-selected" to respond to my survey (which was posted on my website) may have been people who were more inclined to stay together and therefore sought a site like mine.

And my personal experience during the past 25 years is that about 72% of those people who have sought my help have stayed married. (I am NOT a therapist, but I've heard from thousands of people through my work.) Naturally, this is a self-selected group - probably more motivated than most by virtue of seeking me out - but it is a hopeful sign nonetheless."

If you've already made the decision to split, I hope it is the right decision for you. Only you can make that decision and be comfortable with it. If however, you have not decided to split, I suggest you take your time and use that time to improve your own chances of a faster and more complete recovery. There is an important caution for you to take to heart. *Do NOT make any life changing decisions until the emotion has abated and you can think clearly*. When that may be depends on you and your own path to recovery. Likewise, *do NOT allow others in your life to convince you to make a rash decision.* You'll get more than enough well meaning but more often bad advice from friends and family than you can handle. They will tell you to "dump the bum" (or bum-ette) or tell you to move out and do this or do that. Just tell them thank you and make your decisions when the time is right for you and based on logic, not emotion. They cannot truly understand what you are feeling unless they've been through it so take such advice with a gracious grain of salt.

Some Keys to Recovery

In general, it seems that there are a few things that have to happen if you are going to recover in a reasonable period of time. Here's another scary thought; most experts and those of us who have been through it agree that recovery usually takes *at least* two years. Unfortunately, recovery can depend to a great degree on your partner's reaction and willingness to help. If your partner, like many, has either left you or refuses to talk to you about the affair, you can count on a more difficult recovery. But, alone or not, you can make it. Here are some of the important things that should happen to help you recover in a reasonable period of time. The order of occurrence is not terribly important but it does help if they come in the following way.

- **Understanding**. It is almost universal that those of us who are betrayed seek an answer to the question, "Why?" I can recall crying uncontrollably asking God or anyone to tell me why the affair happened. Understanding what went wrong in the marriage, what pulled or pushed your partner into the affair and the details of how it developed is critical to finding a new path to healing. As awful as it may be to consider, our actions may have played a part in your partner's decision (but remember it is not your fault!) and we must know how we should change for the future. A conscious choice by a partner to have an affair can never be excused, it is their choice and not our fault but sometimes our actions make them believe we have put them in a position where they feel wronged and therefore justified. This is an unrealistic view, but most of them see it that way. Don't let anyone tell you that you caused the affair, including your partner who will give you ten thousand reasons why everything is your fault.

- **Closure**. In the case of a couple that stays together, the closure must come in the form of an absolute ironclad end to the affair. Your partner must end the affair so that there is no question as to its end and must be willing to be fully honest as to their activities and whereabouts.

  This is one issue that if not done, MUST result in separation and/or divorce. Don't hang around if your partner continues to have an affair. They simply want their cake and to eat it as well. Let them eat cake, but don't be the one who serves it up to them. There can be no compromise on this unless you want to have what used to quaintly be called an "open marriage."

  In the case of a couple who divorces or separates, the closure sometimes is simply just that they are gone and the marriage is dissolved and you have to begin again, without their help. For couples that do not stay together, the closure is often just an understanding that an affair happened and the end of the marriage.

- **Confession and Apology.** They must have a full and honest contrition for what they have done. They must be truly sorry and show through their actions and words a sincere acceptance of their own responsibility and a willingness to atone for what they have done. If they continue to blame you or fail to admit their part in the affair, you'll never be able to completely rebuild the relationship. And don't rely on promises or words only. Their actions must be what speak the truth. If all you get are more empty promises, it will not help at all. My own wife, after well over a year finally realized the extent of pain and damage to me and our relationship she had caused and made a heartfelt apology to me. More importantly, she promised to take actions that would "prove" to me that she was sincere and has since been very open and honest. She keeps me well informed about her activities and checks with me often. She has shown a great deal of affection and it has been her actions, not her words that have made a difference.

- **Lack of Revenge** or "in kind" action. You must find the strength to avoid harmful actions against your partner. Vengeance, hate and destructive anger will only drive a larger wedge between you. If you have children this is critical. Children love both of you and it causes them much pain to see either of you hurting the other. Control yourself and you'll be in control of your own future. Lose control and you get nowhere. Remember this; the best revenge will be your recovery, with or without their help. You will feel a great deal of pressure within yourself to run out and have an affair yourself to "show them." Not a good idea. Just resist the urge and don't let them drag you down to that level. If you take the high road you will feel much better in the long run.

- **Mutual respect**. Sticks and stones break bones and words DO hurt, sometimes more than the stick. The offending partner is the key person; their attitude and actions must support recovery. Without this, your recovery may be more difficult and possibly longer, but you *can* heal. One respected marriage expert (Dr. James Dobson) attributes almost all failed or troubled marriages to the lack of respect for one partner by the other (or both).

- **Restoration of your own self worth and image.** The betrayal of infidelity does an indescribable amount of damage to our view of our self. Where once we may have been confident and comfortable with our self image, afterward we feel terrible about ourselves. We feel ugly, rejected, undesirable, incompetent and worthless. After all, the one person in our life we loved so much found someone else more appealing. Don't let yourself down, you are not that bad and later in this book I'll help you try to see that. Shortly after discovery, I made this entry in my journal:

  > "I've told her over and over that I feel rejected, humiliated, worthless and emasculated. I've told her I need her affection and approval yet; she still often rejects my advances."

  Even four years later, I struggle with my feelings of inadequacy and low self esteem. This will be one of your most difficult personal struggles.

- **Acceptance and a commitment to yourself to heal.** You unfortunately will at some point need to accept what happened and try your best to overcome it. It will take time. Don't defeat yourself by allowing the situation to constantly bring you down. It may be hard to believe right now, but the time will come when things will be much better. You may even find that life is better in many respects after you've recovered. It is necessary after your initial grieving to commit to yourself that you will try to recover, not wallow forever in your self pity. In spite of saying you should move on, I am not suggesting the unrealistic approach by a famous but I think overrated and misguided relationship "expert" who often says to just "get over it." Such advice is meaningless without some ways to deal with the very real effects of such a trauma. Very few people are able to just "tough it out" without some help. If you are that sort of person, good for you but most of us are not. For now though, go ahead and wallow, cry and grieve for the loss you have suffered. You have a right to feel bad, just don't carry on forever. However you should realize that it can take you two or three years or more to reach a level of "normalcy."

All this is a tall order and I'll give you the bad news right now; *it will be rough*. You probably already guessed that. You'll make some progress and then just as you think things are going well, you'll have a relapse. There will be days you'd rather die than get out of bed. There will be days when the pain will be so intense you'll be desperate and there will be days you'll cry till you think you can't cry any more and then you will cry some more. The whole process of recovery is like a roller coaster, up and down but over time the hills get less high and the valleys become less deep and ultimately you level out. That's where the good news comes in. One day you'll look back and realize you have recovered and are able to carry on a normal loving life and live without pain.

You'll never forget, but you'll be at peace one day and enjoy life again. It may take you several years to reach that point so be prepared for a long and arduous trail. It's shameful that one person's act of selfishness can do so much damage to another person but there is now nothing we can do but try to heal ourselves and regain a happy life. There is no other choice that is reasonable; not suicide, not staying forever in pain, not wallowing in our misery for the rest of our life. You owe it to yourself to gather the strength to recover and find happiness again. For though we have said some acts of revenge are not a proper response, overcoming the pain they've caused you is the best possible reprisal you can deal them.

It also is worth saying that in cases where the partner refuses to cooperate or help you heal, you CAN heal yourself. It will be more difficult and perhaps you'll never have some of the answers you want or deserve but you will be able to recover. If you do end up with an uncooperative partner, you can get some excellent advice and techniques from Phil Delucca's book **The Solo Partner**. For more information about that book see chapter 19 in this book; "The Best Books."

Personal Issues and Obstacles to Recovery

If you are like the rest of us, you are facing a number of issues or feelings that must be dealt with and overcome before you can truly heal. I was so confused and so overcome by emotions and conflicting thoughts after I discovered my wife's affair that I was overwhelmed and had no idea where to start. I looked for answers and it seems as though it took forever to sort out what I was feeling and how to deal with it. In my case, and probably yours, there were some issues that were causing the most pain or were more important than others. Obviously, *feelings such as suicide, self-destruction, homicidal or dangerous impulses demand*

*your immediate attention and must be addressed now. If you
are having such thoughts, as I said earlier, seek immediate
professional help.* Other issues will have varying degrees of pain
or urgency associated with them and can be placed in an order of
priority for attention. In this section you will begin plotting out
your own priorities and I will guide you to resolving the issues
that hurt the most or will give you the most relief.

The result will allow you to quickly find some relief and clear
your mind as you gradually make progress to recover from this
horrible situation. I'll briefly describe the feelings or impulses you
are dealing with and help you determine which are the most
important for you and which will provide the most "healing
power" for you. From that, we'll point you to specific help and
resources in this book to help you recover.

There are common issues and obstacles to recovery that all of
us face in some form or fashion. Not everyone has all these issues
while others have them all. For each issue, rate the "pain factor"
and importance to you of each of these issues. From this
assessment, you can then sort out the most important issues to
you and work on them. In essence, you will break down this
overwhelming problem into components that will be easier to
address and will lead to your own freedom from the pain and
disability that the affair has brought to your mind, body and soul.

- **Suicidal thoughts, homicidal tendencies or
  dangerous impulses.** Some of these thoughts come out of
  anger and depression and are discussed in those sections as
  well. However, these thoughts can be so dangerous that I
  want to address them separately. I have to confess that my
  first thoughts after the despair of discovery were an intense
  anger towards my partner and her lover. I'm not a violent
  person but the intensity of these violent thoughts was
  shocking.

Fortunately, I did not beat my wife to a pulp but I did grab a gun and headed to the home of the lover. I was so outraged I intended to shoot him, castrate him and leave him to die in front of his home. Fortunately, by the time I got to his house I realized how stupid that would be. I also had serious thoughts of killing myself to stop the pain and at one point turned the gun on myself. These thoughts are unfortunately common but most subside quickly. If you have these feelings for more than a fleeting moment, you must seek immediate professional help through a psychiatrist or counselor. Don't let someone else's action end your own life! Don't give them the satisfaction of seeing you go to jail or burying you so they can enjoy life with you out of the way.

If you are having lingering strong suicidal or self-destructive thoughts it is nothing to be ashamed of. But, **contact a counselor, suicide help line or psychiatrist for immediate help; now!** I know I incessantly repeat that throughout this book, but your well being and recovery to lead a happy life is your and my only concern.

- **Anger.** This one is a given. I'm speaking now of non life threatening anger. We ALL react to an affair with anger. It is among the most common and predictable reactions we have after discovery of an affair. The anger can be a slow burn or a very explosive and visible reaction. The amount of anger can be in a range from mild to intense and it can reveal itself rarely, sometimes, often or constantly. Intense and uncontrolled anger can interfere with your daily routine and those around you. Anger can block communication and push those near you further from you. Anger can prevent a reasonable discussion of the issues and shut down any progress. I know you're feeling it, the question is, how much does it block your progress and interfere with your own healing?

If you are feeling intense anger over your partner's betrayal and the anger is spilling over into your daily life and activities you could be hurting yourself and others whom you love or need in your life. If your anger is close to causing you to take physical actions against your partner's lover you must seek help immediately. Don't fudge now. If you truly are having these thoughts it is nothing to be ashamed of. Contact a counselor or psychiatrist for immediate help. Get into an anger management program. Don't let what happened put you in jail or someone else in the hospital. My anger was so intense at one time my wife called the police. I went to jail. If you've never been cuffed, arrested and booked, this is not the time to try it. I guarantee you that if your partner calls the police regarding possible domestic violence, someone will go to jail and it will not likely be them. The police take those calls seriously and even if you did nothing physical, it is likely they will arrest you. I had done nothing except scream at her and bang, there went the cell door. The charges were later dropped and the record expunged but it was a terrible and humiliating experience.

As I already mentioned, on the day I discovered my wife's affair, I was so blinded by anger that I drove to the man's house with a revolver. My intention was to kill or maim him, no lie. I was not thinking straight at the time but by the time I got to his house I had cooled down some. I sat there for at least 30 minutes thinking about what I was doing. I know that if he had come out the door, I would probably be in prison today. I tell you that and repeat it here so that you know that the feelings you may be having are not uncommon. But, I urge you now to not let someone else's stupidity ruin your life anymore than it already has. Don't give "them" the satisfaction of seeing you go down with the ship.

I believe that anger is similar for all of us but have also observed that generally speaking, women and men tend to deal with it somewhat differently. Men tend to take their anger to levels of hostility that can be physical and sometimes result in damage to property or persons.

Women tend to turn their anger inward surprisingly on themselves or they simply hold it in and let it seethe. Turning anger to hostility is foolish and dangerous, turning it inward is damaging to your own health.

Intense anger is a common result of the frustration and pain from a partner's affair. It is one of the most difficult issues to overcome and will take an incredible amount of self control. If anger is your most pressing issue, read chapter six soon.

- **Depression.** You are probably thinking; are you kidding? What normal person who has been dealt this sort of blow would NOT be depressed? After my initial shock and anger, I sank into a deep and desperate depression. No, not the kind where you are just sort of in a funk, this was the kind of depression that robs you of your joy of life, your will to go on and erodes your health. If you are depressed over this affair, welcome to our world, almost everyone ends up with depression. The question is whether or not it is keeping you from functioning. It's ok to be sad, it's ok to feel no joy, and it's ok to cry till you think you can't cry anymore, we all have gone through that.

  But, if you go to sleep and can't get up or you sleep all day just to avoid facing life, you need more help than you alone may be able to give yourself. As with many of these issues, if depression is destroying your life or threatening your livelihood, seek professional help. There are many very effective treatments for depression and you owe it to yourself to look into and use them. See a Doctor or Psychiatrist. With their help you can eliminate deep depression as an obstacle to healing. For more help on depression, see chapter seven.

- **Self Esteem.** As I've said before, the damage that an affair can do to your self esteem is almost incalculable. As an example, here is one thing I said in my journal:

  "As for myself, I feel that I'll never regain my manhood, my personal pride or belief in myself. I know that I was not enough for her and now feel second rate. Of course that will always hurt. I don't want to make love because I'm afraid she'll be thinking of (sex with him) and I'll never be good enough for her again."

  You are probably having similar thoughts and maybe worse ones. My first advice for you to consider on this subject is to not allow her/him to define your value based on his/her own inability to control their own urges. It is not YOU that is defective, it is more likely THEM! It's almost a given that the rejection that an affair imposes on us causes us to feel inferior. If your partner has not already convinced you of your undesirability (remember, It's not your fault.) you'll begin convincing yourself. Never listen to that inner voice that defeats you. After all, if I were better looking, slimmer, more lovable and able to please them surely she would not have done this. Wrong! You could be the most beautiful person in the world and it can happen. Just look at the case of Jennifer Anniston and Princess Diana. Just read the news and you'll see it has nothing to do with looks or worthiness. It has to do with *their* lust and weakness and *their* lack of self esteem. After all, a good screw by someone who tells you all the right things can bolster anyone's self esteem. In fact, if you really think about it, THEY are the ones who have a real self esteem problem and they are trying to pass it off on you. And while you are considering this, you may find that most of the people that partners have affairs with are actually not better looking, in many cases they are dogs. If you are feeling really bad about yourself, read chapter ten.

• **Obsession.** This has been the most difficult and lasting issue for me to personally overcome. In some respects, after over four years, it is still an occasional challenge for me. The good news is that it is now rare and I am able to banish obsessive thoughts quickly. By obsession I mean constantly thinking about what happened and worse yet, seeing it in your mind. I cannot count the number of nights I lay in bed seeing my wife having sex with the other man. It would torture me not only at night but by day also. I called these imaginations my "visions" and they were horrible and so painful it was almost more than I could bear. I'd cry and wail and weep some more all the while trying to get the images out of my head. The more I tried, the worse it became. I was, well, obsessed with what she had done and could not stop the horrible visions. Here are two other raw entries from my journal about this issue, I'll warn you, it does not get any worse than this:

"My mind was tortured with visions of her fucking him and his cock in her and her sucking his dick. (She told me mine "tasted bad.")".

In a later entry I said:

"I was being tortured by horrible visions of her fucking and sucking him. My heart was breaking. On the one hand I wanted her but on the other was disgusted to get

near where his dick had been. I felt unclean and
unworthy. I felt second rate and inadequate."

And in yet another entry I said;

> "I was tortured by visions. Throughout all of these days, I
> was in so much pain that I could barely function. I cried
> 10 or 20 times a day and sometimes could not control
> myself. I would blank out and get really mean again and
> say horrible things then the next minute I would want to
> hold her. This is all so confusing."

No matter how bad it is, remember, you are not alone.
Obsession is one of the most difficult issues to deal with and if
you are suffering with this kind of intense obsession my heart
goes out to you. As much as I hate to say it, this is one of the
areas where drugs helped me immensely. If you cannot do it
alone, (and who wants to suffer alone?) connect to a support
group and consult with your doctor about chemical help.
Unfortunately though, this is an issue that is going to be very
difficult to overcome. But you will be able to do it. If this is
your demon, see chapter eight.

- **Shock and Stress**. I've mentioned more than once the
  shock of discovery and likened it to a mental nuclear
  holocaust. There can be no doubt that such an occurrence can
  cause post traumatic shock and stress beyond belief. There
  were days when I walked around in a fog, unable to think,
  unable to function. I was literally in shock. The stress I felt
  was like none I've ever experienced in my life. There were
  days that I thought my chest would burst or my brain would
  blow up. I was tense, shaky and felt more pain than I though
  possible from stress alone. This kind of shock and stress can

maul your health and spike your blood pressure to dangerous levels. It can render you completely incoherent and dysfunctional. Unless you get a handle on it you might have a complete breakdown or lose your job and everything else that is important to you. If this is a serious problem for you, be sure to read chapter nine.

- **Regaining Trust.** This is a major issue for all of us and one that will stay with you for a long time. Once someone slam dunks you like this, it's very hard to trust them. Worse yet, you probably feel you'll never, ever trust *anyone* again. All of us who've been so betrayed learn that we become very distrustful of almost everyone, especially those who want to get close to us. It becomes particularly problematic if later you try to find a new relationship. On the one hand, we've learned some very difficult but valuable lessons about trusting others. But, the negative side is that too much distrust can prevent us from ever developing a loving relationship again. If you are still with your partner and they make obvious efforts to "make up for" what they have done and to be honest, it becomes easier. In spite of that, you'll find it very difficult to trust them again. Trust though is the most elemental foundation needed for a long term loving relationship. If you are having serious problems with trust, read chapter eleven.

- **Other issues.** Unfortunately, the effect on your life and emotions even goes beyond all the issues I've laid out so far. It may be impossible to cover all possibilities as we all tend to react somewhat differently. But, aside from the other obstacles mentioned, there are some others that most of us seem to have to deal with. One is the fact that from now on "special" dates will become much less special and often the cause of depression or anger. Your anniversary, the anniversary of D-day, birthdays, holidays all take on a completely new meaning and can be very painful. Associated with this is the concept of triggers.

A TV show that plays on adultery, a movie where a partner is cheating, songs, books and all manner of media can include passages or images that cause all the pain to come to the surface. I've walked out of movies or changed channels many times, then cried as the pain all came back. Finally, there is the issue of sex again. If your partner was sexually involved with someone else, your view of him/her and sex with them radically changes. This is a very difficult issue and not at all easy to overcome. For more discussion on these issues, read Chapter twelve.

The Role of Friends and Family

The role of your friends and family can be a two edged sword. It's important that you have people that you can talk to who can support you but it's also important that they do not force choices on you or judge you. Only people who have experienced what you are going through can truly understand your point of view. Sometimes friends and family who have never experienced it will act on incorrect beliefs (that we also had before) and will offer well meaning but remarkably bad advice. As such, you'll need to be very deft in handling the pressures that they may apply.

You may find that your partner's family all take up for him/her and make you a pariah. Often family will defend the indefensible just because it is a family member. Right or wrong, they will agree that you are the one at fault and will believe all the lies you and they were told about you causing the affair. If that comes to pass it will be very hurtful and about all you will be able to do is stay away and let them collectively ignore reality. If you are lucky or they are able to look at things rationally, you may find them a source of support and they may work with you to help you rebuild yourself or your relationship. But, don't count on it.

Your own family will probably be very supportive and sympathetic. Or, in what has been a surprise attack for some of us, they may actually join your partner in blaming you. Be ready for this as it can be very distressing. There is a tendency for some people to always see adultery as a failure of one partner to meet the needs of the other. If this happens to you, try over time to educate your family to understand the true nature of infidelity and your partner's role in making very poor decisions. Above all, don't argue or get belligerent if possible. Once this is over your family will still be a part of your life and will no doubt love you despite what has happened.

Your friends are probably going to staunchly support and defend you. In doing so they will offer all sorts of advice, most of it will be bad. The most often heard advice will be to "kick him/her to the curb." It's easy to say and a common reaction for those who don't really understand. They will also often suggest methods of revenge and ways of "getting back" at your partner or your partner's lover. Ignore them, do what you personally feel is right and do your best to resist the pressure of friends' and family's advice. Listen to them courteously and in some cases, if they are really insightful, they may actually give some good advice but always make your own decisions.

Journaling, Reading & Healing

I've mentioned in passing the issues of journaling and reading as ways to heal. In terms of first aid for a bleeding heart, these tools are the salves that can help sooth the pain. They also help you process things in a more logical way.

Journaling is an often prescribed activity by counselors and psychiatric professionals as a way to deal with much of the mental conflict and emotion associated with any life altering experience. Dealing with death, terminal illness, divorce and betrayal all are often eased through journaling. There seem to be many benefits associated with journaling that not only help purge unhealthy emotions but also allow you to see visible evidence of progress in your healing.

My own journal of despair is titled, "Nightmares and Tortures" and was begun almost immediately after discovery day. It runs to well over 200 pages and is probably one of the most raw and steamy diaries ever written. It rivals the most sordid porn (as you've seen in some of the sample entries I've included) and would probably earn a multiple x rating if ever made into a movie. It is both depressing and exhilarating but shows the progress I've made over a four year period. So what value is that? For me it has been a major element in my ability to cope.

On those days when I knew my heart would break and I could not stand it anymore, I would purge my emotions and pain on paper (electronic). On those days when my anger was reaching dangerous levels it gave me an outlet. My journal was the friend I most needed but did not have. It was a place where I could bare my soul in safety and without fear of being judged by anyone but myself. I could rant, rave and say things I'd never dare say to anyone. There were days when things were so unbearable that I could not get to the computer fast enough to write my thoughts. Somehow just doing that was soothing. The emotion would be spent on writing and the rage was assuaged by just expressing it.

As time went by, my journal became my encouragement and evidence of progress. I would often go back and read early entries and compare them to my later entries and I could see that despite what I was feeling at the moment, I really was making progress. This is an important point because in the fog of pain and sadness, you sometimes feel as though you will never be whole again. Seeing your progress provides hope and assurance that indeed you are healing and the day will come when the journal will be a historic document to either be burned or saved as a reminder of what once was. It does provide encouragement and incentive to go on.

As one website (journalingtools.com) states on their home page:

> **"There's magic in journal writing!**
> Journaling is one of the most powerful tools for self-growth. Simple but effective, **journaling can help you:**
> - **release pain,** frustration and negative emotions like anger and fear;
> - **clear confusion** and make good decisions more easily;
> - **grasp valuable insights** that clear blocks and move

you forward;
- spark your **innate creativity**;
- uncover and nurture a **bigger picture** for your life;
- **reach new heights** in self empowerment."

Believe it; every word is true. I can't say enough or urge you enough to start journaling today. Of course, you'll want to make sure that your journal is well protected from prying eyes. Mine is double password protected (access to the computer requires a password and the file has a different password) and I know that if I should die tomorrow, no one will likely ever be able to access it. Paper journals are not always so easy to protect.

I've also mentioned reading as a method to heal and want to say more about that now. During my earliest days in searching for comfort and answers, I managed to find three excellent books that helped me begin to understand what had happened. The books also allowed me to see that I was not a defective person and to objectively look at what was happening. Books provide insights and understanding that we cannot always discover for our self.

If you are an avid or even casual reader, you already know that reading is in many respects an escape. If you are reading your mind becomes more focused and logical. The emotions you might be wrestling with seem to be set aside and you find yourself in the mind of the author. In the case of novels, you are often transported to another place and time which in and of itself is a wonderful escape. In the case non fiction, the words take you to a place where your mind is guided with clarity to understanding of issues related to the nature of the book. I keep a rolling library of books for new members of our support group to borrow. We all urge each other to read and have all found that reading is some of the best therapy you can find.

Peggy Vaughan, author of **The Monogamy Myth** and founder of the Beyond Affairs Network says it best in her article on the value of reading on her website at: dearpeggy.com/reading.html:

"When you're under the stress of the emotional impact of an affair, your thoughts seem to be out of your control and your mind jumps around or dwells on the same things over and over. Even talking about your feelings can lead to more (understandable) obsessing about them. But getting your mind in gear through reading the words of others can help move the process along rather than leaving you stuck inside your own head."

Read, read, read and then read some more. That said I need to caution you that there are some great books out there and then there are some exceptionally lousy ones. In chapter nineteen I've provided you with my list of choice books that I think are the most helpful and scholarly books based on solid research and understanding of affairs.

Another source of reading and also interaction with others in the same boat as we are is the Internet. If you have a computer and are an active surfer as I am, you've probably already Googled the keyword "affairs" to death. In doing so, you've no doubt discovered that there are hundreds of sites out there. Just as is the case with books, there are good sites and lousy ones.

Unfortunately, on the net the lousy sites dominate the subject of affairs just as they do on just about any subject. Anyone with a computer can set up a site either for free or for peanuts and become an instant publisher. Regrettably, I've seen some really stupid advice and annoying inaccuracies on many sites so be very discriminating in taking advice or assuming what you read is useful. To help you sort out this morass of misinformation, chapter twenty provides a list of some of the more helpful and ethical sites.

Unanswerable Questions

You have probably already asked yourself or others what seem to be unanswerable questions as a result of this betrayal. One of the members of my local support group asked a series of questions that I think most of us have already asked ourselves. Perhaps much of this is second guessing but finding answers to what happened is one of the most essential elements of recovery. Here are his questions and my feeble attempt at answering them for him. First, I'd like to you read the questions and just think about them. As you read them, I suspect you'll be startled that they are so relevant to your own feelings.

Why is it that we all have to go through this hell?
Why do we have to make these difficult decisions?
What is the purpose of it all?
Are we being taught some kind of lesson?
If so, does anyone really know what that lesson really is?
Love, hate, (They are) not really that different now that I am experiencing this whole mess.
Why do you love someone so much you hate them?
Does the hurt ever really stop? Does the pain that digs deep within your chest ever go away?
Is it possible to ever live happily again or I now I wonder, for the first time?

What are these feelings used for?
What is the meaning behind it all?
Why can't we just be numb to it all?
Why aren't there any real answers to any real questions?
I want to die. (Not a question of course but a common feeling.)

Does that all sound familiar? These are the sort of soul searching questions it seems everyone asks when faced with the devastation of an affair and any other devastating life challenge. They are the essence of what we experience when we are betrayed by someone we love. I've asked them myself and actually, though you may not think so, there are answers to each and every question, it's just that we often either cannot find the answers or it takes a long time to do so. Death, cancer, loss of love and other circumstances seem to bring out these kind of questions. They are almost universal in their application to life's miseries.

Here are my answers to these questions; I hope you find them helpful.

"Why is it that we all have to go through this hell?"

Unfortunately, the human experience and life on earth is filled with tragedy and pain. Some people escape the level of pain we are feeling, others share it with us. Though we all ask, "why me?" the real question is often "why not me?" If you have faith, you'll know that this life is full of challenges and that what awaits us is an existence free of these worldly concerns. You've not been singled out but I know there is no comfort in that. Life is a gamble and sometimes we roll "craps." It's what we do after a bad roll that makes the difference. You've not been singled out and you are definitely not alone in experiencing this situation.

"Why do we have to make these difficult decisions? What is the purpose of it all?"

Again, that's life. If it were not this decision, it would be some other that is difficult and painful. Imagine the decisions that others have to make about life and you'll see that it is a part of life and till we are in heaven (or whatever you believe in), there's going to be days you'll have to eat a shit sandwich. As for purpose, some would say that it builds character, makes you a stronger person and brings you closer to God. If you don't buy that, just consider that *the purpose is what you personally make of it*. The purpose can be to defeat you, break you as a person and ruin your life or it can be to indeed bring greater strength and victory over adversity. Believe it or not, you can come through this a better person and live a better life. Yes, it's not the best way to grow but like all things, what you make of it is your choice.

"Are we being taught some kind of lesson? If so, does anyone really know what that lesson really is?"

I've asked that question so many times in the past. A corollary question is; "What did I do to deserve this?" The answer is that it is not that God or anyone else punishing you but that lessons really can come from such experiences. We are being taught a lesson but not one directed by some higher power. As with the above, the lessons learned are mainly up to you. Only you can (and will) find the ultimate answer or learn the lesson. The lesson may be to not trust people as much, or it may be to behave differently in future relationships (or in the future of the current one). The lessons can be many but only you can find them and use them to make your life better.

"Love, hate, not really that different now that I am experiencing this whole mess. Why do you love someone so much you hate them?"

I've heard it said that love and hate are the most intense human emotions there are and that they are only divided by a hairsbreadth of emotional difference. In my case, I managed to sort out that I always loved my wife, still do and probably always will but hate what she did, not her. It was her choices, her actions and her treatment of me that I hated and still do. But through it all, I loved her. It's not that you love your partner so much that you hate her or him; it's probably more that you hate what they did so intensely that it is overshadowing the loving feelings you have (or had). You'll always hate what they did and how they have treated you. In addition, because the hurt came from someone you love and trusted, the hurt is all the more painful and generates so much intense emotion.

"Does the hurt ever really stop? Does the pain that digs deep within your chest ever go away? Is it possible to ever live happily again or I guess, for the first time?"

All I can say is, yes it gets better, much better. All of us who've been through what you have are also finding our way. It just takes a long time. At the stage you are in, it seems to you that there is no light at the end of the tunnel. We are trying to show you the way and telling you that you can love again, live again and feel joy again. You'll always remember this terrible experience and there will always be scars but the pain will become dimmer and life will be brighter. You'll be a different person, but you'll recover. I've been in the process for a long time and I now have many more happy days than sad, much more laughter than tears and on almost every day the clouds over my head part to let the sunshine in.

Consider this a storm, the storm of your life that lasts for two years or more but trust us, it will pass, if you will let it!

"What are these feelings used for? What is the meaning behind it all? Why can't we just be numb to it all?"

The feelings are only natural, as with the above, the meaning is there for you to find or fashion for yourself. As for being numb, we all wish that. Not to be flippant about it, but I will tell you that drugs help tremendously. If you have not considered that, see a doctor and talk about your depression and hurt, there are things that can help. You won't be numb but at least you won't be debilitated by the pain.

"Why aren't there any real answers to any real questions?"

There are, it's just going to be hard work finding them, and you will eventually. I've not found all the answers yet, and may not till I move on from this life, but little by little, day by day clarity has come and so does the peace of understanding and acceptance.

"I want to die."

I can't tell you how many times I've said that myself. I can tell you I've heard it from just about everyone who's been through this. I can only repeat what I said to you before; don't let them take away the most precious thing you have; your own life. You'll survive and I dare say you'll be glad you did not die. Hang in there and don't let someone else's actions define your life from now on.

We're all pulling for you. We all will give you whatever strength we can to help you through this. YOU WILL HEAL and enjoy life once again. But, so much is up to you to help yourself and find the way. Hopefully I and the others who have faced this challenge can offer you our own experience and ideas but in the end, you must find the way that is best for you.

Dealing with Your Anger

After the initial shock of learning of a partner's affair, most often the first emotion to overwhelm you is anger. Your anger will be directed at your partner, your partner's lover, yourself and just about anyone or anything nearby. It's ok, but please don't beat the dog. If you have one, he or she will be the one "person" in your life right now who will love you with honesty and no conditions. My dog was the only anchor I had during the weeks after discovery and I would have been much worse off without her. It's not a bad idea to get a dog if you don't have one. They will be a source of love and joy. For the short term, anger can overshadow just about every other emotion as you try to deal with the awful revelation and the betrayal by someone you trusted and loved. Many people speak of having murderous thoughts after discovering an affair, some let the anger control them and carry through. Others manage to wrest control back and think logically.

Just about all the books will tell you that anger is "natural," and expected in such circumstances. Some counselors and advisors will tell you anger is good, some will tell you it is bad, some will make you feel guilty for being "out of control," and others may fuel the fire with encouragement. The answer lies, as with many things in life, somewhere in between. Anger is such a strong emotion that it can however, take you down paths that could destroy you.

One book, *Torn Asunder* by Dave Carder (see our review of this book in chapter 19) says anger is the natural response —indeed the healthy response." Anger is healthy? He goes on to say that getting mad can result in good. He tells us that there are positive as well as negative results of anger.

Things to think about: (It may help to write your answers for all the questions we pose) Note also that if you need some help with the questions in this and the following chapters, the Appendix starting on page 199 offers suggestions and some commentary on the possible answers or purposes of the questions.

What good do you think comes out of anger?

What negative consequences are there?

Peggy Vaughan says (dearpeggy.com):

> "After discovering a partner's affair, the strong emotions often take over and dictate our actions - even when we try to control them. This can feel overwhelming and lead to believing there's no way to either understand or change this pattern. However, it is possible to understand why it's so hard to get control of our emotions - which, in turn, may help make it possible to actually get control of them."

So, how on earth can you get control of these strong feelings and save yourself from a state of constant anger? It is not easy! Understanding a little about it can possibly help. Peggy quotes a rather dry scientific study that gets deep into the physiology of anger. Here is a part of it:

"It's necessary to learn to recognize the feelings that accompany the emotional state. Tightened muscles and a sick sensation in the gut, for example, typically accompany fear, while rage is characterized by an upsurge in aggressive energy and increased body temperature. Learning to readily identify an 'emergency' brain state via its characteristic physiological signals is the first, crucial step - because brain studies suggest that the moment you become aware of your internal state, you activate the prefrontal lobes, which in turn, can begin to moderate your response. So it's important to try to notice any changes happening in the body and intensely focus on the bodily changes rather than on the thoughts that trigger them.

"The next step is to support the effort of the 'thinking brain' to consult with the inner defenders of the 'emotional brain' about the possibility of letting down its guard. Since the hair-trigger defense system of the emotional brain is such that for many couples, learning to regulate brain states is all but impossible in each other's presence, it may be necessary to be alone in order to calm down long enough to do the kind of quiet, deeply focused work that is necessary to allow an emotional system to shift. (dearpeggy.com, quoted from an article "The Emotional Imperative" By Brent Atkinson)

Great, what does that mean in English? It simply means that the best way to deal with intense anger is to recognize what it physically feels like when you are getting angry and stop and think rationally. One of the books I have in my personal library, *The Solo Partner*, said it best. "

When we are angry, we revert to a reptilian state that is ruled by the need to attack our prey. I call it my "Alligator Me."

The book goes on to say that as soon as you feel the alligator coming out, bring the human back into the picture and take control by becoming more rational and in control. That single bit of advice has helped me more than anything in controlling the destructive kind of anger that further damages a relationship and friendships. You must learn to recognize the feelings that accompany growing anger and don't let the alligator take over.

Think about this:

Do you know the signs of when your alligator is taking over? (What physical and mental feelings do you have when you begin to get angry?)

Write them down then think of ways you can trigger your human brain or head off the animal reaction. This is all well and good but what about that under the surface, seething anger that just seems to stay with you and won't go away? Are there ways to get past that and turn the alligator into a nice pair of shoes or a purse? One major contributor to unresolved anger is what Dave Carder calls the obsession cycle. Here is how he illustrates it.

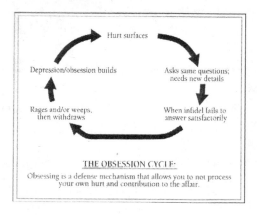

From *Torn Asunder*, pg. 155, with permission.

It's hard to get past this cycle but it's worth it if you can recognize it and get yourself going in more productive directions. Carder also speaks to a Depression Cycle that also can keep anger alive long after it has served any useful purpose.

More points to ponder:

What productive ways have worked for you in the past to process or reduce your anger?

What advice would you offer to others who are dealing with anger?

(For possible answers to these questions and all the others in this chapter and the following ones, see the appendix; "Example answers to questions" on page 199)

Now take your own advice. Here are some of things the experts say will help you process and resolve anger:

When dealing with an outburst of anger:

- Breathe deeply, way deep down; breathing from your chest won't relax you. Imagine your breath coming up from your "gut."
- Repeat calming words or phrases such as "relax," "take it easy." Repeat it to yourself while breathing deeply.
- Visualize a relaxing experience, either from your memory or your imagination. Remember that day at the beach with a

Corona in one hand and Jimmy Buffet's music playing on your Walkman.

- And yes, you can count to ten, twenty or whatever it takes to divert you.

Longer-term ideas:

- Instead of an outburst of anger, go straight to your journal and divert that energy into writing about what made you angry.
- Maintain your journal and be sure to note times when you are most angry or hostile. Doing so will help you better understand your anger patterns and what triggers your anger most often.
- Seek the support of important people in your life in coping with your feelings, cultivate trusting friendships and talk with them about your anger and feelings.
- Try to find more constructive ways to use your anger energy. For example, if you find yourself angry at another person, try to explain to them what is bothering you and why. It takes more words and work to be assertive in this way than it does to let your anger show, but the result is worth it.
- Learn how to laugh at yourself and see humor in situations. Humor can be a great healer.
- Don't deny your feelings, feel them for yourself and let them run their natural course (but don't let your alligator take charge).
- Make an "anger list." Write down all the things that make you angry. Get them out of your head and then discuss them with your partner, a friend or God. Discover ways to eliminate the sources then check them off. Just seeing some progress can help you.
- As you look at your journal and anger list, honestly look at the sources of anger that come from within you or from your own

actions. Pledge to yourself to change to make your own life better.

I view anger as an unexpected and usually intense burst of energy that you can either use to your advantage or not. Sometimes that energy is so powerful you need an immediate physical outlet. If you can control yourself long enough to put on your running shoes, take a run or a walk. Jump on a bike and pedal like hell. If you have exercise equipment, use it then and you'll get a great workout to expend that energy to the point where you find it hard to be angry, at least physically. One member of my support group did just that and not only did he calm his anger by diverting that energy but as a bonus, he lost 100 pounds (he needed to.)

I know that much of your anger will be directed towards your partner and their lover. A great way to expend that personal and potentially harmful energy is to get a photo of them and take a stick, ball bat or whiffle bat, go to a far corner of the house, and proceed to beat the heck out of the photo. Yell, scream, call them names and beat till the picture is pulverized. I have done that with a picture of my wife and a wedding photo of us and it honestly helped me a great deal. It's useful to get all that negative energy out and this is a great way to do so without really harming anyone.

Dealing with anger can be very difficult and frustrating. Even though I know the "pre" anger feelings quite well, sometimes I just cannot stop myself from reacting or lashing out. I always feel terrible after I do. In spite of that, I feel I make progress little by little in controlling my alligators and taking things less personally and more cordially. All of us who have experienced what you have fully understand how you feel and know how difficult it can be. You can overcome this. If you try these suggestions and your anger still is not abating or even getting worse, see a counselor or find an anger management class that you can attend and get support from.

Whatever you do, avoid taking your anger to the physical level involving your partner or the other person. That may land you in jail or worse. For men, this is more difficult as it seems our genes are always directed towards the "fight" rather than "flight." But it is so critical that you not do that. If you feel yourself headed that way, call someone, take a drink(in moderation), take a pill, do anything other than take it to a level where someone will get hurt. In the long run, you'll be the one to pay the price.

If nothing you try seems to help much then be sure to seek professional help. See a counselor, a pastor or enroll yourself in an anger management program.

Dealing with Depression

Depression and the desperation that often accompanies it is one of the most common afflictions we experience after the discovery of a partner's affair. Sadly, it is also one of the most common conditions that adults suffer from regardless of affairs or not. According to the National Institute of Mental Health (NIMH):

> "In any given 1-year period about 18.8 million American adults, suffer from depression. The economic cost for this disorder is high, but the cost in human suffering cannot be estimated. Depressive illnesses often interfere with normal functioning and cause pain and suffering not only to those who have a disorder, but also to those who care about them. Serious depression can destroy family life as well as the life of the ill person
>
> Most people with a depressive illness do not seek treatment, although the great majority—even those whose depression is extremely severe—can be helped. Unfortunately, many people do not recognize that depression is a treatable illness."

Many of us may believe that depression is just a sad mood that will pass. Sometimes it does if it was only caused by a temporary event. However, when it lasts, some sort of action is necessary to help us recover from the depression. In other cases, a permanent condition may be present called clinical depression that is only made much worse by the devastation caused by a partner's affair. For those of us who have been betrayed, the depression usually sets in not long after discovery. Initially you'll be so delirious with anger and other emotions it won't have time to grab you but once all the initial emotional energy starts to ebb, so enters depression.

One expert says that it does not matter whether or not your depression is short-term "situational" depression or "clinical." He says, (mhsource.com) "Depression is depression is depression." at whatever point you are suffering from depression, "you have it." In fact another site (psychologyinfo.com/depression/) states that *any* period of depression becomes clinical in its effects and treatments.

Depression changes your very life. It changes how and what you eat, how you interact with others, how you think, how effective you are at work, your energy level and how you feel about yourself. Depression is not "feeling sad," over an incident where the sadness goes away in a few days. Nor is it a time when you are tired or discouraged or under temporary stress. It is longer-term situations where these feelings linger intensify and begin to interfere with work, school or family responsibilities.

Things to think about:

Do you think you suffer from a form of clinical depression?

What symptoms are you personally experiencing?

Symptoms of depression.

If your list of symptoms includes several of the ones listed below (taken from the NIMH site at nimh.com) you may be suffering from clinical depression. If so, you should seriously consider seeing a mental health professional.

- Persistent sad, anxious, or "empty" mood
- Feelings of hopelessness, pessimism
- Feelings of guilt, worthlessness, helplessness
- Loss of interest or pleasure in hobbies and activities that were once enjoyed, including sex
- Decreased energy, fatigue, being "slowed down"
- Difficulty concentrating, remembering, making decisions
- Insomnia, early-morning awakening, or oversleeping
- Appetite and/or weight loss or overeating and weight gain
- Thoughts of death or suicide; suicide attempts
- Restlessness, irritability
- Persistent physical symptoms that do not respond to treatment, such as headaches, digestive disorders, and chronic pain

Not everyone who is depressed experiences every symptom. Some people experience a few symptoms, some many. Severity of symptoms varies with individuals and also varies over time. Unfortunately, a partner's affair can bring on every one of those symptoms. It did for me and for many of the people in my support group. If you are suffering from depression, you may not just "snap out of it." There are some things you can do for yourself but often professional treatment is needed. I suggest you at least talk to a medical or mental health professional if your life is being limited or negatively affected by continuing depression.

What can be done to treat depression?

Without getting all wrapped up in a treatise on psychology, there are basically two ways of treating depression; psychotherapy (or counseling which is a form of psychotherapy but sounds less threatening) and drugs. Within each of these two arenas, there become more options. NIMH says:

> "There are a variety of antidepressant medications and psychotherapies that can be used to treat depressive disorders. Some people with milder forms may do well with psychotherapy alone. People with moderate to severe depression most often benefit from antidepressants. Most do best with combined treatment: medication to gain relatively quick symptom relief and psychotherapy to learn more effective ways to deal with life's problems."

What we are facing in dealing with an affair and the aftermath is very often a cause of what the National Depressive and Manic-Depressive Association say is a major depressive episode (MDE).

> "For example, let's suppose someone develops a MDE in the course of a divorce. Psychotherapy may very well examine the meaning of marriage for that individual; feeling loved versus feeling abandoned, etc., and perhaps relates these issues to the individual's past response to similar traumas. But the general approach to the patient is the same whether there is, or is not, a clear incident that is the cause of the MDE. In more severe MDEs, medication is often necessary. "

But, they also go on to say:

> "This is not to say that everybody who is feeling upset or
> down in response to a psychosocial stressor is clinically
> depressed, or in need of professional treatment. Many
> individuals reacting to such stressors will do fine simply
> by getting support from friends, family, clergy, or even
> on-line chat groups. Some will find solace in self-help
> manuals or non-professional support groups. <u>But when
> the person presents with a full-blown MDE, especially
> when accompanied by suicidal feelings or ideas, he or she
> should seek out a health care professional.</u>"

More Questions:

**At what point would you consider seeing a psychiatrist,
counselor or physician to help you with your
depression?**

**How do you feel about using prescribed drugs to treat
your depression?**

**Besides these options, what have you been able to
personally do to make you less depressed?**

From my own experience, the drugs prescribed for me have a few
annoying side effects but nothing that can't be adjusted to or dealt
with. Most have a significant number of possible side effects and

you should carefully consider the side effects and talk them over with your doctor or counselor. They'll give you guidance. For those of us who are somewhat fragile with regard to our sexuality, be aware that there are some sexual side effects. Those are most often a lowered desire and a reduced sensitivity resulting in delayed orgasm. I've been on anti-depressants and sleep aids for four years now and they have really helped me personally cope with my depression and feelings of well being. They've also helped me with some intense panic attacks and anxiety. Though I feel they are helpful, recent studies (issued January, 2008) have put the true efficacy of some of the anti depressants in question. Those studies are in dispute but insinuate that the act of taking them and the expectation of improvement is what is effective, not the drug. As for me, I'm sticking with them because I honestly can feel the difference if I forget to take them.

You can also find a lot of on-line resources that relate to the way these drugs work and the side effects. Some people prefer using herbal or homeopathic drugs but the effectiveness of alternative treatments have not been proven. Some research has been done that indicates a success rate of around 25% for a few of the homeopathic remedies. In looking at a number of sites related to homeopathic or herbal treatment of depression, almost all have disclaimers that their treatments for "a transient episode of depression, homeopathic remedies can be useful in alleviating the blues." At least one M.D., Dr. Jay Gordon at drjaygordon.com, suggests use of "Gingko Biloba or Borage. He says that "there has been a good amount of success with a combination of the two as well."

I know this all seems like a bleak outlook, but in spite of it all, there are things you can do to help yourself along. One method that has had success is called "Cognitive Behavior Therapy." The basic premise of this is that how a person thinks directly affects how the person feels. I believe that is very true. It is the self-fulfilling prophecy syndrome and that has proven to be very real. Within the context of depression, how people perceive themselves is critical to recovery or not. It is important to say uplifting positive statements over, and over again. This can be done in a mirror, through written exercises, or the individual can tape his/her own voice and play it back to get maximum effect. Statements such as:

"I am a capable and lovable person."
"I can deal with the situations presented to me today."
"Right now, I feel good about myself."
"I love the direction my life is taking."
"I can deal with any difficulty that comes up in my life."

can help you counteract the "other" voice (or ex) that keeps telling you otherwise. I'll have more to say about this in the chapter on self-esteem. In addition, as NIMH suggests, friends, family and support groups such as BAN can significantly help you deal with depression. Just seeing that other people are experiencing the same feelings and in many cases, seeing their success can be uplifting.

Sometimes depression can make the smallest tasks seem impossible. One way to deal with this problem is to break the task into smaller parts. Sometimes even the simplest tasks can be a chore. It may seem like a lot of work just to get out of bed in the morning. But if this broken down into small steps, it can be accomplished. Start by sitting up, and then put your feet on the floor. Keep it up till the task is completed.

Helping others and expanding your own world is really

helpful. You can do this by getting involved in church activities, volunteering in any capacity, or just getting involved in a community group. This can help to distract you from your own problems, and give you a sense of self worth and demonstrate that you really are a good person and can accomplish good things.

Exercise is a wonderful healer. Vigorous exercise produces endorphins. These body chemicals produce a euphoric state. This is especially helpful to the depressed person who may have a deficiency in serotonin, another mood enhancing naturally produced chemical (many of the drugs address this deficiency). Exercise gives you more energy, assists in weight loss, and stimulates a healthy appetite. All of these benefits directly affect specific symptoms of depression. It works with depression just as it can with anger and other destructive emotions.

There are many other lifestyle activities that can help you such as; aromatherapy, reading books, dance and movement, meditation, music, pets, just plain fun things like a picnic or a funny movie and relaxation therapy (how about a good massage or some Yoga?). Finally, a change in diet can help. Moderation in alcohol, avoid sugar highs and eat generally in a healthful way.

If in spite of this you still have bouts with depression (regrettably, the odds are good that you will) make sure you have some friends nearby to talk to when you need a lift. Of course a Beyond Affairs Network support group can be a very good lifeline.

Dealing with Obsessive Thoughts

Sometimes, actually quite often, individuals dealing with the stress and anxiety caused by an affair form intrusive thoughts that relive the pain, anguish or details of their partners affairs. For many of us these thoughts come in the form of thinking of our partner having sex with his/her lover and imagining what they did when together. When these thoughts first began to haunt me, they were so graphic; I labeled them "visions."

According to many experts, obsessions are "normal" thoughts that become exaggerated with increased frequency, duration and intensity. Everyone has unwanted thoughts some of the time. Focusing on and worrying about these thoughts makes them stronger. A scary aspect of obsessive thoughts is that very often, people carry them out but in most cases, they do not. For example, obsessive thoughts about harming the partner's lover do not mean that you will really carry the idea out. It may help you to know that 99.99% of us felt the same way. Obsessions do not have anything to do with your character and morals or what is really happening or about to happen in your life. It's easy to say that obsessive thoughts don't really mean anything - they are just static from the brain. It's harder in practice to ignore them. Do not judge yourself because of the obsessive thoughts and don't study them for some sort of message. Anxieties as well as other events like lack of sleep stimulate obsessions; poor diet, lack of exercise and stress can also stimulate anxiety.

There can be no question that the discovery of a partner's affair can bring on anxiety and obsessive thoughts, and in a very intense way. It stresses your life in every way possible and you become paranoid in your worries and concerns. This issue has been the most difficult thing for me to overcome. I can tell you that from my support group and hearing from readers like yourself, obsessive thoughts are a major issue for many of us. These thoughts can cause you to constantly relive your worst nightmares and "see" what your partner has done over and over. It is a bit like a recurring nightmarish version of the film "Groundhog Day."

Questions for you to consider:

Do recurring undesired thoughts related to your partner's affair haunt you?

What are some of your most recurring obsessive thoughts?

Here are some expert observations of obsessive thoughts and tendencies:

"Obsessive tendencies tend to be based on your stage of life, environment, and even season of the year. Most people with obsessive tendencies do not totally eliminate that part of their personality, but it is possible to reduce the obsessions in strength and frequency so that they are not so bothersome."

"Taking compulsive action to try and take away the obsessive thoughts only tends to make them stronger. Think of obsessions like quicksand. Analyzing the obsession simply makes it worse. The more you focus on them, try to figure them out, struggle against them, etc. the worse they become. Remember that obsessions are not really important. Instead, visualize the obsession like a small cloud - notice it and then let it drift away. Realize that obsessions are of no real consequence - they are "just brain noise".

That is of course nice from a scientific point of view but the real question for us is; how can we keep these thoughts from destroying us or causing more pain? How can we turn them away?

As always, the experts have many good suggestions that can help us overcome obsessive thoughts. Interestingly, most agree that willpower alone, trying to push the thoughts out of your head, *only tends to make the obsession stronger.* Our main task in dealing with obsessions is to separate ourselves mentally from them. Yes, we have obsessive thoughts, but *we are not our thoughts.* A good way to start this process is by writing down your obsessions in list form, rating their intensity, listing what comes before the obsession (A trigger) and what comes after the obsession. Pay close attention to any things that you experience or do that tend to come right before an obsession goes away. Sometimes you can accidentally find things that will help you chase them away.

More questions:

What are some of the triggers that start your obsessive thoughts?

What have you personally done that seems effective in controlling your obsessive thoughts?

One important thing you can do to overcome your obsessions is to shift your focus and then *relax*. That is easier said than done for many of us! Another surprising idea from the experts is that seeking reassurance from other people just makes an obsession stronger - or at the very least does nothing to confront the anxiety surrounding the obsession! They suggest that you handle your obsessions yourself. I can see the truth in that. If for example you go to someone and they are sympathetic and offer many condolences, they are actually in some ways extending the experience rather than helping you stop it. However, I believe that a support group of similarly afflicted people such as the Beyond Affairs Network can provide you with additional strength and encouragement. It's true that too much sympathy can prolong the feelings but understanding and support from other people who have experienced what you are going through can be very helpful.

It is important that you be aware that anxiety causes obsessions to appear. Developing active methods for anxiety reduction tends to reduce obsession. Give yourself the opportunity to feel the anxiety that comes up when you are confronting an obsession. This is very important. If you do not give in to an obsessive thought your anxiety is almost certain to rise. This is normal. Watch the anxiety and allow it to be there. It will gradually drop over 20 to 60 minutes and this is how real positive change happens. Some of my anxiety attacks (I called them panic attacks) would last for way too long for comfort. I guess I am weaker than most people for again my Doctor prescribed anti-anxiety medicine and that really helped me get past the worst incidents till now I almost never need any help and have very, very few obsessive incidents.

If you are tempted to obsess about a feeling, thought, or other item allow yourself only a few seconds to think about it. Then redirect your attention to something closely related (e.g. another body sensation or feeling). Then try to redirect your attention to something else you would like to do or think about. By making multiple leaps from subject to subject, you get mentally further away from the obsession. Obsessions are "projections" of your self into the past, the future, other people and situations. They are more imagination than anything and in many cases they are just a reflection of your worry, not reality In most cases you must remember that THEY ARE NOT REAL, your mind has manufactured them. Try to focus on the present and what you are doing and this can diminish the power obsessions will have over you.

Sometimes obsessions can appear because you are holding back your true emotions. If you think this is the case, find a safe way to feel and express feelings (tears, anger, fear, grief, etc.)

Focus on the positives in your life rather than the obsessions and what might be "wrong". A good way of doing this is by making a list of positive things that occurred that day that you are thankful for. Provide yourself with rewards and positive feedback for any and all progress dealing with obsessions. Remember, obsessions can be very, very strong and powerful. Take care of yourself, be nice to you. If you are having trouble getting free of an obsession, get out of Dodge. Take a day off and go to the beach, grandparents, visiting friends, hiking, or to just get away from any persons and places that trigger your obsessions. Keep track of progress you are making and remember the experiences that give you relief. Saying "No" to some expectations tends to lead us away from obsessions. Freedom of choice and listening to our own desires opposes obsessing. Keep in mind some helpful words and phrases: Relax, Back off, get real, Let go, Accept. It's ok to have things be imperfect. Lighten up! Say "So what!" Live in the present.

Something I recently learned from someone in a discussion forum was what he called the "glad" game. It bears some consideration. Basically it is a bit like the idea that if you get lemons you make lemonade but it is more fun and can be done as things happen to you or feelings come to you. The way you play is to simply think of an alternative that could be worse. So, for example, if you have an obsessive thought about your partner and the other person being together, think of something that might be worse and express it as a "I'm glad that" phrase. In this case you could say, well at least I'm glad that this is only my imagination. By the way, this can be a fun game in life in general. The next time you see a rude and stupid driver, you could say, "gee I'm glad he doesn't drive near me all the time" or "I'm glad he did not run over someone." You'll find that the glad game can really help with anxiety, anger, obsessions and many of the more aggravating things life dishes up to you.

Here are several additional techniques for overcoming obsessive thinking.

1. If you find yourself obsessing simply shake your head as if you were shaking the thought right out of your head. It sounds stupid but sometimes it works.

2. When you notice yourself obsessing actually shout; "STOP" in your head (or out loud) and then move on to another activity or direction. This is different than trying not to think about an obsession - which only makes the obsession stronger. Instead it is interrupting the obsessive process.

3. Develop your own list of the worst fears you obsess about. Read the list out loud and record it if possible. Then listen to it and be objective. Laugh a little at the absurdity of some of your thoughts and let your anxiety pass. I think you will see that some of the things really are not worth worrying over.

4. Place a rubber band on your wrist and snap it when you notice yourself obsessing. This is another seemingly dumb idea that really works.

5. Back track some of your obsessive thoughts to see what started it. Maybe you can learn more about what triggers them and avoid those thoughts in advance of the obsessive thought.

Think about which of these techniques do you think will be most helpful to you? Try them all and you'll hopefully find several that will work for you.

The above content facts and suggestions for dealing with obsession (excluding the discussion questions) were adapted from an article by Christian R. Komor, Psy.D., a clinical psychologist.

This issue is of such universal concern and affects many of us so profoundly that I've also added some important thoughts from Peggy Vaughan, the founder of BAN.

From "Triggers" - Images, Memories, Flashbacks" by Peggy Vaughan:

> "The recurring images of your partner with someone else are tough, especially since they come back for quite a while - but they can/do eventually go away. How well I remember the way I'd be lying in my husband's arms, then suddenly have this sinking feeling just sweep over me, as I'd imagine him with other women in his arms.
>
> I found that anything/everything could trigger those images. His very first affair was with a woman whose name was the same as our daughter's middle name - so there was no escaping that. And as silly as it sounds, I even found myself affected by the fact that our family dog reminded me of one of the women - because they both had red hair!
>
> The images and memories don't just magically disappear, but they do eventually diminish and then gradually fade away - if you work at helping that happen. While we can't keep them from coming, we can refuse to "dwell" on them; we can immediately try to move away from those images.
>
> Also, of course, the way we're being treated by our partner during our "recovery" can make a big difference. If we're able to balance these painful images with new, more positive experiences, it helps enormously.
>
> Finally, just a reminder that I'm not talking theoretically here, I've "been there" and struggled with the images as well, but they DID go away and I have no

residual pain from them. So I thought it might be helpful to share my own early struggles.

Here's an excerpt from Peggy's book, Beyond Affairs:

"The memories continued to haunt me. I'd be doing just fine, and then something would happen to remind me of the past - and it would feel like it was happening all over again. The least little thing might trigger these memories. It could be a reference to a particular person or place or subject, or a color or a song - or a hundred other things. Invariably, it would bring back in full living color every detail of the painful feelings and events of the past.

This yo-yo up and down in my ability to cope with his affairs continued to keep me off balance for two or three years. There were times when things would be great and I'd think I was over the hump and had adjusted. Then... Bam! I'd get knocked all the way back down into a depression.

I frequently wished I could have amnesia. That seemed to be the only way I could forget the past. Also, I wished for time to pass. I'd always heard that time heals, but I never heard just how much time it takes. I didn't know whether I could last long enough.

We spent many, many hours talking about our feelings and trying to get a handle on the whole experience. Little by little it got easier to handle the emotional aspects too...Finally, one day the pain just slipped away when I didn't even notice."

From Peggy's "Question of The Week Archives."

How can I deal with the triggers?

Here are a couple of questions about this very common problem.

Question #1:

It's been about five months since the discovery of my husband's 6-month affair with someone that I thought was just a friend of his. We are in therapy and every time I think we are making progress, something triggers all the anguish and heartache all over again and I fall back into depression and panic attacks. Last night it was an episode of *Sex and the City*. I just don't know how much longer I can stay on this emotional roller coaster from hell.

Question #2:

How is it best to deal with triggers? I was recently looking at photographs taken during the time of the affair. When we took the pictures I was so happy. Now the sight of my partner smiling in the photos really makes me worry. What can I do to get over it?

Peggy's Response:

This is a fairly pervasive problem--dealing with "triggers" that serve as ongoing reminders of the affair. The thoughts, memories, or a flashback to a time when our partner was intimate with someone else seems to be an inevitable part of the process. And when people are in pain over a partner's affair, it feels like it will never end.

While we can't prevent these thoughts from coming, we can make a difference both in their strength and their duration--if we refuse to feed the thoughts when they do come. There's an old saying that "what you feed is what grows." So when these thoughts come, if you give in to them, go over and over the incident in your head, dwell and obsess about it for quite awhile--it only grows stronger.

Instead, when the thoughts come, you can deliberately focus on shifting your thoughts away toward whatever (anything) more positive about your current life or the prospects for the future. Of course, this is not magic and won't "work" the first time--but consistently shifting away instead of going deeper into the thoughts will gradually rob them of their power to create pain.

Since it's unrealistic to think it's possible to just "not think about it," the goal is to get to the point where thinking of the affair doesn't trigger the same painful emotions. This process involves gaining as much information and perspective about affairs as possible in order to allow the rational understanding to become stronger than the emotional reactions to the thoughts about the affair.

How do I stop obsessing about the affair?
Question:

How do you stop obsessing about the affair, the third party and the situation? We are almost at the 1-year mark of the affair. We are working and seem to be doing well but reflecting on what went on a year ago leaves me lost and angry. Some days I can 'forgive' but some days I am devastated with memories. As the 'anniversary' of all this approaches all my good efforts seem to be for nothing.

The shock, anger and pain are as strong as the day I found out.

Peggy's Response:

The process of personally recovering from this experience is a very slow, jerky one. I've often repeated that it takes at least two years to fully recover from the emotional impact--even with the best effort by both parties. And during that time, there will be many ups and downs. On any given day, you may (as expressed above) feel "as strong as the day I found out" and feel it's hopeless that you'll ever recover. But there are no doubt other days when it's much better, and you feel very hopeful that you're "on your way" to recovery.

So one of the keys to not getting too discouraged is to recognize and acknowledge the jerky nature of this process. It's normal, expected (even inevitable) to have this roller coaster, yo-yo, in emotions. But there should be a gradual diminishing of the number of times and the intensity of the feelings associated with each "down" time. So it's important to be patient with yourself as you go through this process.

However, it's not a case of simply sitting and waiting to feel better. The process of gradually lessening the down times is not completely out of your control. You need to constantly work to get more rational understanding (about affairs in general and your situation in particular) to help offset the power of the emotions. This involves reading everything you can find about the subject and talking about it, both with your partner and with others who can be supportive.

Also, while you may not be able to avoid being struck by the feelings of "shock, anger and pain," you can have some influence over what happens once you get those feelings. On the one hand, you can give yourself over to the feelings--and the "obsessing" that can accompany them--by reviewing every detail over and over in your mind, in essence reinforcing the feelings.

Or, you can deliberately move away from the feelings by distracting yourself with other thoughts or activities. This "distracting" must be planned in advance. Go ahead and determine what other things you can do or focus on the next time you're struck by these feelings--so you're prepared to go into action when the next attack strikes.

Peggy Vaughan's "Questions of the Week" archives are a wonderful resource for you to get answers to many questions beyond what I've addressed in this book. Hundreds of questions about affairs and recovery from people like us have been carefully answered by Peggy over many years. The archives are for sale on Peggy's site at her bookstore. I urge you to check them out at: dearpeggy.com/shop/questions.html. By the way, all excerpts from Peggy's books and website throughout this book are used with permission from her.

Dealing with the Shock and Stress; the Trauma of an Affair

Note: *The purpose of this chapter is NOT to imply that you are afflicted with PTSD or to diagnose it in any of us. The purpose is to look at the physiological and mental effects of a shocking occurrence and to learn more about how stress affects some people and possible ways to cope. Under no circumstances, should you allow this chapter to cause you to diagnose any specific disorder, for that you must see a professional health care provider.*

After I discovered my wife's affair, I was in a state of shock. I could not think clearly, my body was in a state of fight-flight and I was besieged by conflicting and complex emotions. At one moment I was angry, at the same time I wanted to make love and then I would be sad and so depressed I was suicidal. It seems the only missing emotion was euphoria. The day I saw my doctor, she told me that I was suffering from Post Traumatic Stress Disorder. Up to that time, I had only heard of PTSD in the context of war or other major disasters. I thought, "how could that be, I wasn't in a war zone." But, was I? Is it possible that the shock of discovery of an affair can rank up there with combat, a plane crash, a tornado or rape? You bet it can, and the damage done to you physically and mentally can reduce you to a helpless incompetent wreck.

PTSD has been around for a long, long time. It is only recently though that it has been named as such and gained a great deal of publicity. Here's how the National Center for Post Traumatic Stress Disorder (ncpstd.org) defines it:

> "Post Traumatic Stress Disorder, or PTSD, is a disorder that can occur following the experience or witnessing of life-threatening events. People who suffer from PTSD often relive the experience through nightmares and flashbacks, have difficulty sleeping, and feel detached or estranged, and these symptoms can be severe enough and last long enough to significantly impair the person's daily life."

Nightmares, flashbacks, detached, no sleep; sound familiar? Another site: (trauma-pages.com) says:

> "Traumatic experiences shatter our assumptions about trust."

The National Center for PTSD goes on to say:

> "PTSD is marked by clear biological changes as well as psychological symptoms. PTSD is complicated by the fact that it frequently occurs in conjunction with related disorders such as depression, substance abuse, problems of memory and cognition, and other problems of physical and mental health. The disorder is also associated with impairment of the person's ability to function in social or family life, including occupational instability, marital problems and divorces, family discord, and difficulties in parenting."

It is interesting to note that according to the experts, women are <u>twice as likely</u> to develop PTSD as men! Though the definition does not specifically mention discovery of an affair, it is important to note that it does indeed bring on PTSD in some people. Regardless of whether or not you have PTSD, we can all agree that what you have experienced is devastating and life-altering and brings with it a tremendous amount of stress. And the stress that follows discovery of an affair can be very intense, as you no doubt know already.

Answer this for yourself:

How did you feel after discovery of your partner's affair and what were some of the "symptoms" or behaviors you experienced?

Here are some of the very real consequences or symptoms of the kind of excessive stress you might have experienced:

- Feelings of fear and foreboding.

- Loss of memory.

- Easily startled, and with heightened reactions.

- Feeling drugged. (There are hormonal changes that cause this)

- Reliance on alcohol.

- Major depression.

- Problems with other relationships and aggressive behavior.

- Headaches.

- Dizziness.

- Chest pain and gastric disruption (heartburn, high blood pressure etc.)

There is an old saying that "you are how you feel," and nothing could be truer in this case. If the feelings brought on by your discovery get the best of you, you can easily suffer major health problems.

Of course, the $64 million question is; "how can I overcome the effects of possible stress disorders and improve my health?" Psychiatrists are somewhat at odds over treatment but this much is known; there is no one treatment or action that works for everyone in every case.

Consider this:

What are some options that you think might help a person overcome stress disorders?

There are basically two ways to deal with stress disorders from a clinical point of view:

1. Talk therapy, that is, counseling and group therapy. Included as an important part of this are support groups such as BAN.

2. Drug therapy, Zoloft, Prozac, and Wellbutrin to name just a few. Drug therapy is most often only a short-term solution unless a person is headed for clinical depression or is already clinically depressed.

But, how else can you deal with stress from a personal, non clinical point of view? Are there ways that you can cope with this incredibly stressful event? Many people either may not want to take drugs so what other options are there?

Think about this:

What has worked for you in reducing the effects of stress on your own life?

If you have some successful techniques, hang on to them and remember to use them whenever you are feeling depressed.

Here are some other tips from the experts:

- **Don't sweat the small stuff,** Try to prioritize a few truly important things and let the rest slide

- **Try to "use" stress.** If you can't fight what's bothering you and you can't run from it, flow with it and try to use it in a productive way. Just as I've mentioned about anger, stress can bring on a surge of energy and if you can, try to direct it in constructive ways such as some of the following ideas.

- **Work off stress** with physical activity, whether it's jogging, tennis, mowing the lawn, gardening or any other physically exerting activity.

- **Do something for others** to help get your mind off your self. This is one of the most revitalizing and satisfying actions you can take. Helping others in your own pain is selfless and restorative to the soul.

- **Learn how to relax yourself.** Meditation, prayer and breathing exercises have been proven to be very effective in controlling stress. Practice clearing your mind of disturbing thoughts. Aroma therapy or sound (white noise etc) therapy may help. If you have a hobby that you can immerse yourself in, do it more often. Look into biofeedback as a relaxation option.

- **Don't overwhelm yourself by** fretting about your entire workload. Handle each task as it comes, or selectively deal with matters in some priority. Remember the old maxim of how to eat an elephant; one bite at a time.

- **Remove yourself from the stressful situation.** Give yourself a break if only for a few moments daily. Go outside, go inside, change location, get a cup of coffee, take a walk do a crossword puzzle.

- **Find** something you can change or control in the situation. If you give it some thought, you'll find that there are many things you can change. You can leave, you can look into a divorce, you can change the way you look at your marriage. There is no need to feel completely controlled by the affair, you do have choices.

- **Avoid extreme reactions;** Why hate when a little dislike will do? Why generate anxiety when you can just be a little nervous? Why rage when annoyance will do the job? Why be depressed when you can just be sad? That sounds pretty elemental but it can help immensely. Just as the "glad game" can help control anger, it can also help you mediate your reactions. Use it here too or just step back and chill out for a moment.

- **Develop a thick skin,** the bottom line is "I upset myself," take your self induced stress out of the picture. This is a recurring issue in almost every one of the challenges you face. You are what you think is so true so do your best to look at the positives and think more constructively. The "glad game" has many uses here.

- **Eat nutritiously and regularly,** This can be a key in not letting stress damage your health. Nearly all of us have found that in the period following discovery we lost our appetite. Most of us also lost weight. For some people it was needed but this method of weight loss is not desirable. If done simply by not eating, you'll lose energy and alertness and become even more helpless. Eat three squares a day and though you may not eat as much, try to make your meals balanced to ensure you are getting the needed nutrients to stay healthy. Though you'll really not feel like it, eat anyway as a way to restore yourself.

- **Connect with your friends,** just getting out and being with someone you trust and can rely on can be helpful.

Find things to do with them; shop, go to dinner, go to a movie, run together and play games or just talk.

Most importantly, if stress is putting you in an out of control state or interfering with your schoolwork, social and/or work life, **seek professional help.** Remember that stress can hurt you in many ways, both physical and mental. Don't just live with it. Do your best to be aware of it in your own body and deal with it. If the personal activities I've suggested don't work, get professional help before you suffer some real harm.

10

Restoring Your Self Esteem

Perhaps one of the most personally devastating results of a partner's affair is the damage done to your own self-image. The complete rejection and devaluation of yourself by your partner is unthinkable and an unexpected shock. Once it hits you, it is like a ton of bricks. You begin to have doubts about everything that defines you. Your worth, your looks, your sexual attraction and ability, your judgment and whom you even believe you are is all thrown into question. All of these things and more make up your own view of yourself; your self-esteem. Remember what I said before, you are what you think and if you think poorly of yourself, you become that person. Are you going to let someone else define you in such a manner? Of course you won't.

The website more-selfesteem.com defines self esteem as: "the opinion you have of yourself. It is based on your attitude about the following:

- Your value as a person
- The job you do
- Your achievements
- How you think others see you
- Your purpose in life
- Your place in the world
- Your potential for success

- Your strengths and weaknesses
- Your social status and how you relate to others
- Your independence or ability to stand on your own feet "

I remember just how I felt about myself in the days just after discovery (and in some respects, even to today). I was despondent and I questioned all the above and felt like an abject failure. I felt unworthy of anyone's respect, most importantly, my own. My partner had shown that she had no respect for me, so why should I respect myself?

Think about these questions:

How did you feel after discovery of your partner's affair?

What sort of thoughts did you have about yourself?

What you were/are feeling is a predictable consequence of the rejection you've faced. We tend to rely on how we are doing in the present and the opinions of others to determine how we feel about ourselves. What we desperately need after such an experience is some positive experiences to offset the negative feelings and thoughts that plague us. Even then, the good feeling can sometimes only be temporary.

All that makes us question how we can find enough positive experiences to offset the horrible destruction that has been brought upon us. Sometimes, we find unhealthy ways to rebuild.

Think about this:

What are some unhealthy ways to try to rebuild?

As hard as it may be to believe or accept at the time, we are not seeing ourselves accurately when we allow someone else's misbehavior or mean spirited attack to become the measure of ourselves. Healthy self-esteem is based on our ability to assess ourselves accurately (know ourselves) and still be able to accept and to value ourselves unconditionally. This means being able to realistically acknowledge our strengths and limitations (which is part of being human) and at the same time accepting ourselves as worthy and worthwhile without conditions or reservations. Stop and think; does this one person's opinion define us? Do one person's actions towards us define our value? Would you accept the words of someone who lies to you, sneaks around and defiles your relationship to be the person who sets the level of your own value? Of course not! And don't!

What else, besides your partner's opinion and actions defines your self worth?

An important part of defining ourselves is our own inner voice. That is the part of you that is critical or self-defeating. It is the self-fulfilling prophesy of success or defeat. How many times has your inner voice criticized you? How many times has your inner voice told you that you would fail at something before you begin? My greatest lesson in this area was in playing my violin. My own fears would defeat me at the start. I would say to myself that I'd probably miss a note, play a sour note and get lost in the score or otherwise mess up. And guess what? I always did. Once I got control of that inner voice, I found myself instead concentrating on success and did much better. It's the same with your life. As long as you defeat yourself, you'll be hard pressed to pull yourself out of this grand funk of low self-esteem. Listening to the negative inner voice can waste energy. Stop telling yourself you are a failure, ugly, worthless or that you won't be successful. Instead start reminding yourself of the good things in you, be positive about success and don't let "them" define you. Change your inner voice to one of positive support and motivation.

Think about it:

What examples can you think of where your inner voice worked against your success?

Is the inner voice always logically correct?

The long-term consequences of low self-esteem go far beyond just the mental anguish. Low self-esteem:

- Can create anxiety, stress, loneliness and increased likelihood for depression and other stress related illnesses.
- Can cause problems with friendships and relationships.
- Can seriously impair academic and job performance.
- Can lead to underachievement and increased vulnerability to drug and alcohol abuse.

Worst of all, these negative consequences themselves reinforce the negative self-image and can take a person into a downward spiral of lower and lower self-esteem and increasingly non-productive or even actively self-destructive behavior. So now, as always, the big question is; how can we reverse the spiral and rebuild ourselves?

Think about this:

What has worked for you to build your self esteem? What ideas do you have for yourself that might work?

Here's what some of the experts have to say that might help.

- Write down everything you like about yourself. (Another good use for a journal)
- Write down things you'd like to change (and can) and work down the list.
- Listen for compliments - and believe them.
- Pamper yourself with new clothes, a massage and a walk by the water, in the park or in some other soothing and invigorating place.
- Join a support group. (BAN, here you are!)
- Seek out people who make you feel good about yourself; a good friend can be worth their weight in gold.
- Avoid the critical types of people, the Mr. or Mrs. Negative. You know who they are so steer clear of them.
- Figure out some things you do well and then do them.
- Stretch your boundaries learn some new skills, try a new hobby.
- Don't be afraid to use the pronoun "I" and use it to say what you feel.
- Accomplish something every day. Every day can be filled with little victories and try to tune in to what you are doing each day. Any accomplishment from the simplest (like doing the dishes) to the biggest is fodder for self praise. Be liberal in recognizing your own accomplishments.
- Treat yourself with respect. You've earned it, especially for surviving this personal hell.
- Define your worth yourself; don't let a single complaint or person define your total worth. Some people build *their* self worth by devaluing others. Remember that whenever someone criticizes you. It may not be you they are really criticizing you as much as they are trying to

elevate their own value. It's twisted but it's true. And also remember that we all mess up from time to time. Take your mistakes with plenty of grains of salt. Look at the whole of you, not just the bad.

- Do not mirror the criticism of your partner or other people in your own mind. You know yourself better than they do and when it comes to your partner, if they lied about having an affair, doesn't it make sense they would lie about you?

A key point here is that you must think positively about yourself and your value. Don't allow someone else to define you!

If you are trying to build new relationships:

- Profit from past mistakes by acknowledging them.
- Don't seek out a carbon copy of your former partner - or an exact opposite.
- Evaluate each person who enters your life as an individual.
- Do everything you can to establish equality in your new relationship(s).
- Consider courses and retreats to prepare the two of you for a lasting relationship.
- Avoid extreme changes in your lifestyle.
- Strengthen ties with friends and family as you move in new directions.

With regard to self-esteem, sometimes you just have to "talk to yourself" in a very positive way or at least get some encouragement. On the following pages are some "cards" that you can cut out and use to boost your self esteem. Just take a different one each day and place it on your mirror or place them all around the house. If there are some you think I've left out or are more applicable to you, make your own cards! They are TRUE and don't let your inner voice tell you otherwise!

Positive Thoughts

I have hope for the future.

I am strong and can over-
come feelings of hopelessness.

This is only temporary .

Inspirations for Healing—Copyright © 2005 Richard Alan

Positive Thoughts

Just because one person rejects me
does not mean everyone will. I'm
confident that there are many people
who will find me very attractive. I
look in the mirror and see the beauty
in myself.

Inspirations for Healing - Copyright © 2005 Richard Alan

Positive Thoughts

I am not a worthless person.
Think of all the loving and
caring things I have done (list
them). I can be proud of what
I've accomplished in life.

Inspirations for Healing - Copyright © 2005 by Richard Alan

Positive Thoughts

It's NOT my fault, I don't
need to feel guilty that they/
he/she made a stupid
decision.
IT'S NOT MY FAULT!

Inspirations for Healing - Copyright © 2005 by Richard Alan

Positive Thoughts

I can control my own future, no one else has control unless I let them. I am not helpless. I'm going to do something for myself today.

Inspirations for Healing - Copyright © 2005 by Richard Alan

Positive Thoughts

I am a dynamo! I'm going to take a long walk, exercise or ride my bike. I won't let what happened take away my energy. Get up and go!

Inspirations for Healing - Copyright © 2005 by Richard Alan

Positive Thoughts

I love life and will not let someone else or a temporary setback ruin the rest of it.

I have so much to look forward to and I'll stop dwelling on past events that I cannot change.

Positive Thoughts

I'm not afraid to find friends or look for love from the opposite sex. I've learned so much. I know I can better judge people and be sure my future relationships are rock solid.

Positive Thoughts

I am a capable and loving person!

Right now, I feel good about myself.

Inspirations for Healing - Copyright © 2005 by Richard Alan

Positive Thoughts

I am sexy & attractive! I'll put on my sexiest outfit and go to a party or a club and enjoy being with people. I won't hide, I'll mix it up!

Inspirations for Healing - Memphis BAN ® 2005

Rebuilding Trust after a Partner's Affair

Rebuilding trust after the betrayal of an affair goes far beyond the issue of trusting your partner. Regrettably it often extends to other people close to us and sometimes to all mankind. A betrayal such as an affair is a very tough lesson to learn about the treachery of our fellow humans. For me the lesson was that you simply cannot put blind trust in someone just because you love them. Try to look at it from a distance. The statistics tell us that upwards of 50% of people in relationships lie, cheat and commit adultery. That means that half the people you meet in this world are likely to betray you. That is absolutely astonishing.

Given that probability, the question you need to ask is not whether or not you trust someone but to what extent. Blind trust is downright stupid yet almost all of us who are suffering through this nightmare are guilty of blind trust, in the name of love.

Once this happens to us, we begin to look suspiciously at others. We wonder if we can ever trust anyone again? We certainly know after discovery that we cannot trust the one who betrayed us. Rebuilding trust with them can be a very long and precarious process. Deciding whether or not to even try is your first obstacle and we'll deal a little more with this subject later. A lot will depend on your partner's attitude and willingness. At this point though, they'll have to work very hard to earn back your trust.

The issue of new relationships is also an awkward process. If we end up ending the relationship with our current partner, dating and building new relationships becomes challenging. You'll have a tendency to be very cautious, even mistrustful. That can be detrimental to the prospects of establishing a relationship. However, that may not be all that bad if handled properly.

Let's face it, trusting blindly and being blinded by love just does not make sense. Being careful and selective does make sense. What you've learned will enable you to be much more critical of others and allow you to "sense" the possibilities of honesty or dishonesty. I don't think I'll need to lecture you here because you already know this. Just keep your "antenna" up and stay tuned in to others. Before love takes you hostage, be analytical and logically assess those you are trying to make friends with.

One bit of good news that Peggy Vaughan tells us is:

> "Getting answers to understand what happened is an essential aspect of rebuilding the marriage, but it is NOT a key to personal recovery (which does not depend on whether or not the marriage survives). Therefore, staying together or being divorced may not interfere with your ability to rebuild trust."

On the other hand; Peggy Vaughan conducted a Survey on Affairs that included a question about rebuilding trust among those who were divorced after the affair. The answer may not be immediately encouraging.

"(Question of those who were divorced after an affair:) Have you been able to trust (people) enough to develop another intimate relationship?

41% - No, I'm very anxious about ever being vulnerable to being hurt again

35% - I've developed another relationship, but "hold back" somewhat

24% - I've developed a new "trusting" intimate relationship "

Peggy went on to say:

"Affairs can have a long-term impact on ANY future relationship. Ending the marriage doesn't end the impact of a partner's affair on the ability to trust someone in a future relationship. In fact, "recovering" from a partner's affair does not directly relate to staying married or getting a divorce. That's because *personal recovery* is separate from *recovering the marriage*.

Some people who stay married DO recover - and some DON'T.

Some people who get a divorce DO recover - and some DON'T.

Here are some keys steps involved in *personal recovery*:

•Accepting the fact that it happened (no more "if only..." or "why me?")

•Understanding the complex reasons for affairs (not *just* "personal failure").

•Deliberately focusing on dealing with it and talking openly about what happened.

•Allowing time to heal.

•Believing it's possible to recover.

Those who go through this process of personal recovery are the ones most likely to be able to trust enough to develop another intimate relationship. And *since this process takes time,* it's not surprising that only 24% of the respondents have been able to develop another relationship following their divorce."

In addition to Peggy's comments, several of the other national BAN support group coordinators have offered these thoughts about trust:

"My experience is that the ones who stay in marriages and their partners are doing their part to rebuild trust, heal quicker and therefore move on more quickly"

"When we discussed this issue (in her group) of 'How do I ever trust anyone ever again?' what came up in the group was a general consensus that we did not trust ourselves. Many felt they had made bad choices in choosing their mate. And, if not that, they felt they had made bad choices in allowing their partner to treat them in disrespectful ways during their marriage. The general consensus among those attending that evening was that the real issue was having trust in ourselves to make healthy choices in how we relate in our relationships in the future."

"You shouldn't just blindly trust anyone. We all have to develop skills in discerning who to trust and when to trust. And we need to judge the behavior and not the words. Trust is a risk to be sure but to not take the risk is to cut your self off from many meaningful relationships. As much as there are many untrustworthy people in the world, there are also many wonderful trustworthy people. Wise people don't cut themselves off from everyone, because of past hurts. They learn to improve themselves, and they learn to recognize who to trust, when to trust and to what degree to trust. Blind trust is unwise and naive."

"Before disclosure of the affair, trust is high. After disclosure of an affair, trust plummets to an all time low. Through SINCERITY (for example, breaking all ties now with the third party) trust climbs perhaps 30%. Through ABILITY (discussing the affair, answering questions and proven behavior during this time) trust climbs another 30% or so. Through DURABILITY (being faithful, open and honest - proven behavior - over an extended period of time) one can regain full trust. It takes time, with work and proven behavior."

(Anne Bercht at beyondaffairs.com/articles/building_trust.htm)

"I would agree that there is probably a little more suffering for those of us who must first be confronted with the infidelity, and then must struggle through divorce (of course, this is no intention to minimize the pain we all go through regardless of the circumstances, it's just that there are so many additional emotions in divorce). I don't know, though, that I could say that trust is a more difficult issue in my situation than in those remaining with the unfaithful partners (I have been through both situations BTW). I think trust is something we will all be struggling with for some time, and in fact, in some ways, my trust issues were easier to overcome without having to actually deal with the individual who perpetuated the symptom. "

"Anyone who's been divorced from an unfaithful partner must first learn to trust themselves before 'exposing' themselves to others, and that, unfortunately as most people know, involves much time. Time has been my greatest healer, and it has been through much time and solitude that I have been able to again trust my ability to recognize those who are good and worthy of my trust. In fact, perhaps we can acknowledge that much good can come from the adversity we have faced in these situations especially for those of us who are "abandoned" after infidelity, because we do learn to better establish boundaries, read "red flag" behavior, and determine that our trust is something that others must" deserve" instead of automatically obtain. I have found that the new instincts (which probably aren't new at all, but just reawakened!) I have developed since D-day regarding whom I should/shouldn't trust has proven to be very useful and accurate, whereas prior to that time, I seemed simply oblivious to those who were treading on my personal boundaries."

What the books and other experts say:

Dave Carder in *Torn Asunder*:

"The initial rebuilding of trust must start with identifying and grieving the losses that have occurred in the relationship. Those are, loss of self respect, loss of boundaries, loss of sexual expression, loss of trust, loss of openness with others, the loss of the world you thought you had."

Don-David Lusterman in *Infidelity, A Survival Guide*:

"Reestablishing trust can be a long and difficult process. There are many setbacks along the way. Admission and remorse (by the infidel) are critical, even if the relationship doesn't continue. Establishing trust is worth the effort, it will give you a better marriage or a better divorce."

Peggy Vaughan in *Recovering From Affairs*:
"Trust depends on facing the fact that monogamy never gets settled once and for all. (It also depends on) Committing to honest communication based on fairness and equality."

Perhaps all these ideas are confusing but at the same time, there are some very important gems of wisdom. In my opinion, and that of many of the people I've worked with in our support group, rebuilding trust is one of the most difficult obstacles to overcome. It is also one of the most enduring and doggedly persistent concerns. Most of us who've been so betrayed tend to think that we will never trust anyone again but the truth lies somewhere in between.

Questions for you to answer for yourself:

Everyone seems to say it takes time to rebuild trust, are there things we do to slow it down? Can we speed it up?

Has your experience given you the ability to better assess the level of trustworthiness of other people? If so, in what ways?

Are there things that you can do as you develop new relationships to assess the level of trust you can put in others?

Looking back, do you think your trust in your partner was blinded by love's emotions? If so, how would you approach a new relationship using what you have learned?

If you are still married, do you worry about your partner having the patience to "hang in there" while you rebuild trust? How can we help them be patient?

A betrayal such as this teaches us important lessons about human nature and the romantic view we have of love and relationships. We all believe our love will carry us through and is strong enough to overcome all. In many cases, for perhaps more than half of us, that seems true. Where our partner gives up and strays, we hold on and stay loyal. Unfortunately for others, it is not enough and they resort to other behaviors. Without judging right or wrong, from this we should know that to fully trust in any human is foolish and terribly laden with naiveté.

Having a healthy respect for human nature and being alert to the signals we see is not a violation of love but simply a necessity in any relationship. For more about trust, see the trust issue in chapter 14, *Dealing with the Betrayer* and also see chapter 16, *For the one Who Had The Affair* to see my advice for what they must do to restore our trust.

Other Issues

Sex & Sexuality Issues

Something that will be extremely difficult for you will be the issue of sex. If your partner's affair involved sex with the other person, sex again with them becomes a very painful and upsetting process. Almost every person in my support group that I've talked with about this issue has confessed to feeling very "dirty" and repulsed by the offending partner. For one thing, none of us wants to be a second choice. For another, the thought of them having wild sex with someone else just does not engender loving intimacy. We tend to look at them as defiled, dirty and disgusting.

It is likely that one of your very first actions after the initial discovery will be (was?) to "reclaim" your partner sexually and have sex soon after. This will be an extremely painful and emotional situation and may even cause you some humiliation afterwards. There is a tendency to want to reestablish your stature as the alpha sex partner and do it soon. If this has happened to you, you probably already feel remorse. Don't, we almost all do it and we almost all feel the same as you do.

If it has not yet happened due to your revulsion towards them, take it easy and do not force things. Some of the individuals in my group went more than a year before overcoming their disgust. If this is the case, it is perfectly ok. If you stay together and your partner pressures you, just tell him/her how you feel in a logical (not attacking) manner and that you need time and space. If that happens you will no doubt worry yourself silly thinking that they may resort to their affair partner to relieve their sexual energy. As bad as it sounds, so what, they've already committed the sin and doing it again can't be much worse. If they do, then you have learned a valuable lesson about their commitment to reconciliation and that can guide you in making decisions as to the future of the relationship.

You also might find that in a reversal of fairness that your offending partner avoids sex with you. This can be very upsetting as you will definitely think they are "getting it somewhere else." It is understandable that you might think that way but there could be other explanations.

Your partner may be very ashamed of what they did and simply cannot bring themselves to have sex. Your partner may also be mourning the loss of their lover and needs time to get over it. Though I want to say "tough noogies," the fact is that this very well could and does happen. At some point, regardless of who is avoiding sex, an open and honest discussion needs to take place. Avoid anger and just be straightforward about your needs and worries. There is a good likelihood that you can work it out and begin to heal sexually much sooner than if you continue to avoid the issue.

Of course there is no question that for a while, sex with your partner will bring a lot of pain and sorrow. If you are like me, you'll often have to battle visions of them with their lover. Sometimes they will come right at the worst possible moment, sometimes immediately after. Try some of the techniques that were discussed in the chapter on obsession or simply look at it more clinically. You need it; they need it so take it as it comes. I can't tell you how many times I had sex and just imagined my wife as a way to sexual release. I often thought it was certainly a better option than a prostitute.

During long periods of sexual drought, don't be ashamed to masturbate and relieve yourself. Men tend to need this more often and some women have difficulty with the idea. Get a vibrator, read a sexy book or watch a sexy movie and have some chocolate. Remember, you may know better than anyone how to make yourself feel good so don't overlook this option. For some of you, religious tenets may cause you to avoid this option, if so, I would respect your position and simply suggest you find other ways to deal with any sexual tension you experience. There is always the "cold shower" method or exercise.

Of course it might go without saying but I'll say it anyway; do not run off and have casual sex, retaliatory sex or sex with a prostitute or promiscuous person. Times are too dangerous for that. I know, your partner was reckless but you have more sense than that! On that subject, times really are too dangerous for casual sex so regardless of what your partner does, immediately get yourself tested for STDs. If your partner really cares about you, they will too but may not. My wife never did and it still bothers me that she cared so little about me to do so.

I'll share a rather humorous story about retaliatory sex from my journal, perhaps it will cheer you up:

> "I really got obsessed with her lack of concern for me and on again off again affection. I printed off some pictures and profiles of some single women looking for men (on the internet) and told her that they wanted to have sex with me and that I was going to meet one of them. I was trying to make her jealous and it almost was if she really did not care. I told her that two could play the same game and since she thought it was fun, I wanted to screw somebody too. I told her I was going to take pictures of us having sex and share them with her. Of course we had a huge argument and I left telling her I was going to have

wild sex with this woman. She called me on the way and we argued some more. She asked me to come home as I hoped she would and so I did. I later told her it was all a fake to make her jealous. However, I have had several women express an interest in me. I had posted my name on a couple of match sites basically saying I wanted a mistress. Three or four have responded but they are all so ugly I'd have to be nuts. Besides, though in a way I want revenge, deep down inside I don't want to do to her what she did to me."

Maybe you don't think that was funny but it is a story I tell often to my people in the support group. In some respects it fulfilled my desire for revenge but without really doing anything very harmful other than antagonizing my wife. I don't recommend you do the same but it actually did make her think about what she had done. This occurred only two weeks after discovering her affair.

Reminders and Special days

One of the most difficult aspects of getting past the pain is the seemingly constant reminders that appear to be present almost daily. You'll soon realize that affairs are a commonly exploited human condition that appears in movies, TV shows, books, even commercials and advertisement. The most classic and offensive example of the latter was the General Motors ad that appeared sometime around 2005 as a billboard advertising "buy one (car) for yourself and buy one for your mistress." That one caused quite a flap among those of us who had been so harmed and they ultimately retracted that campaign.

You'll find reminders everywhere. They will appear in books, magazines, commercials, TV shows, movies, radio and even in actions you see between other people. It will drive you to distraction and probably anger you as well. For me, the most annoying TV show at the time of first writing this book was ABC's *Desperate Housewives*. ABC is quite proud of the program and touts it constantly and now "me too" shows are cropping up. Here we have a program that exploits marital unhappiness and adultery and elevates it to the level of legitimacy. Hog wash! But, it did not end there. Recently, a new show has taken it to greater and more disgusting heights of bad taste and voyeurism, "Lipstick Jungle" is NBC's newest entry in the irresponsible bad taste sweepstakes. They are simply disgusting!

I've often wondered if any of the people involved in these shows have personally experienced the pain we are feeling as the result of an affair. I'm sure they must have yet the activities continue. The main reasons are obvious. Money, sex, lies, deceit and adultery sells. Americans (and some other cultures) have a morbid curiosity about other people's troubles. A sordid affair makes for top selling news, magazines and shows so if one is in that business, it seems to be a must. The hell with morality or ethics, money is the driver. So now here we are, faced with this onslaught of reminders that can ruin your day, almost every day.

Aside from my own soapbox rant, it's more important to know how to deal with this attack on your senses and emotions. Now, you're going to say "DUH," but I have to say it; just ignore it and when you can avoid it. Of course I know that is naive and simplistic but let me explain how you can do that.

First, you should try your best to accept the fact that it will not change and you can not change the global view. You can of course, sell some other individuals on the moral and ethical issues related to exploitation but there will always be those who exploit it for personal or corporate gain. You'll never get Jerry Springer or Maury off the air. They will always exploit other people's misfortunes and marital wanderings as it is the nature of their business and their viewers love it. It is strange how Springer can be both the worst show on TV (by his own admission) yet tuned in to by millions every day. Maury is equal or runs a close second but plumbs different depths of moral and ethical depravity.

Beyond that, we can learn from them that there is an element of our society that feeds off your misery and does not give a damn how it affects you. Accept that and don't waste your time trying to "educate" them. Instead, educate those closer to you and ignore those who exploit our misfortunes. Have pity on them for their lack of sensitivity and their greedy ways. Then forget them.

Try to realize that they are not personally targeting you, just the general situation. Don't take it personally. Don't patronize shows, movies or companies that support them or exploit adultery for their own gain. Turn your back on them and use your feet to protest. When you do encounter such a reminder, try your best to remove yourself from the situation. Walk out of the movie, throw away the book, turn off the TV or leave the area. If it makes you feel better, go ahead and write to them to express your feelings but don't expect a response. Even though I've said to not try to educate some people, expressing your dissatisfaction can be very cathartic. Despite my advice, an organized writing campaign can actually change some things. That's what happened in the case of the offending GM advertisement. Many people wrote to them from our BAN support groups around the world and the ad was withdrawn.

I did write a letter to ABC's *Good Morning America* host Diane Sawyer over their constant celebration about how great *Desperate Housewives* is. Of course I was ignored but at least I felt better telling them off.

So turn away, ignore them, have pity on their stupidity. If you still find yourself affected, try some of the "stop obsessions" actions outlined in chapter eight.

Special days in your relationship will also be very difficult for you. Anniversaries, birthdays, special holidays will all be reminders of happier days and break your heart. The anniversary of "D" day will be especially difficult as it seems for at least a couple of years, that day will be a reminder of the horrors you faced on discovery and the nightmare that you life became for weeks after.

In spite of that, we still must cope. In the hopes that it will provide some comfort, here is a Christmas message I once wrote to my group. I realize that many of you are not Christians and I hope it does not offend you to read this. I simply ask that you look at it in the context of your own beliefs and look at the concepts behind the message. Also, think of it in the context of other important holidays and dates, the concepts are the same.

"So many of us face Christmas and other important holidays with sorrow and pain for the loss of someone we loved (or still love) or for lost dreams and hopes of a lasting family. For some of us, it is may be our first Christmas in a world turned upside down by a partner who betrayed us and seemed to care more about themselves than us or our families. For others it is an ongoing struggle and a reminder of the pain and loss.

Christmas for most people is about faith but what of the faith and trust we had in those we love(d)? They betrayed that faith and trust and left us with an emptiness; a hole in our heart that seems as though it can never be filled.

How can we face these holidays alone or with such a burden that is so heavy you feel as though you can never lift it or get out from under the load? It's funny how some of the most joyous times of the year can be so painful. For one thing, the holidays bombard us with images of lively and healthy families, all reconciled, all reunited. (Ho, Ho, Ho). That can just inflame our feelings of hurt and desertion. As one person said;

"I remember one very tough year I just kept seeing myself standing at the manger, a pilgrim with other pilgrims, burying my face into the hay surrounding the Christ child and just softly whispering "Help."

That is how I feel, I just want to cry out for help but it seems that it has not come my way. I have stopped wondering if I'll ever feel joy at Christmas and just want to find peace. Perhaps you feel that way too.

It is a shame, for the season and Christmas should be the most joyous time in each year. As Andy Williams sang; "It's the most wonderful time of the year." It is the time when good will to men is the watchword.

Yet still, the pain makes it so difficult to be joyous. I know that you may feel that way too. I wish that I could take your pain away. I wish that I could lift your burden but I cannot. However, in some measure, I hope that our fellowship and partnership in understanding helps all of us find some comfort. I know that being with the people in my support group has helped me immensely. So what can we do? Here are some thoughts:

- Focus on the joy of the season or holiday; take comfort in the true meaning.
- Let us not let those who have hurt us take away that which once brought us joy. They destroyed our marriage but did not destroy the meaning of Christmas or other holidays.
- Find new meanings for the season, make new memories with those who you still trust and you know you can depend on. Remember your children, your parents, your siblings, cousins and closest friends, they did not deceive you and many of them are still there for you.

- When you look at a symbol of Christmas, let it take you over, not in sorrow but in its true meaning.
- When you hear a Christmas carol, sing along and remember your childhood and singing those carols in school, you may be the last generation who will have those warm memories.
- Think of the smells of Christmas, what wonderful nostalgia they bring. The smell of fresh cut balsam, of mom's pumpkin pie cooking, of cinnamon, holly and spiced cider. Those joys are with you still and always will be.
- Think of each of us who are suffering the same pain as you are, remember that you are not alone and there are people who understand and care about you and want you to find peace and freedom from the hurt.
- Eat yourself silly, stuff your face till it hurts then laugh and giggle over it.
- If you are with kids, make Christmas about them; lavish them with love, presents and fun.
- Walk around your neighborhood (or any one with lots of lights) and enjoy the beauty of it all.
- Call someone you care about but have not seen for years, tell them how much you miss them and wish them a Merry Christmas.
- Go to a party, crash one if you have to and have fun with people who are your friends.

The bottom line is that we should all try to find new meanings and joys for special holidays and dates. Trying to forget is impossible but trying to recall the other things that make that time of year or day special and make new memories can make the season or date a happy time again. I pray that you find peace, happiness and joy for these days and every other day of your life."

Forgiveness as a Part of Recovery

Forgiveness is a subject that comes up quite a bit in discussing recovery from infidelity. While in our daily life, offenses against our partners are common, and the offender usually wants to be forgiven, infidelity rises to the top in terms of relationship offenses. While we all tend to forgive minor offenses, in the case of infidelity there is usually a great deal of reluctance to forgive, particularly if the offender hasn't learned anything from the ordeal. Some books will tell you forgiveness is necessary for you to move on. Other books will tell you forgiving adultery is good for you. And others still will lay out processes and form letters that will help you heal.

In my experience, though forgiveness of the offense may help one become whole again, I've seen many cases where forgiveness was not possible in any formal way and still the offended partner was able to move ahead. I place this chapter here to present several sides of the issue and you can make up your own mind as to the value and necessity for forgiveness.

Forgiveness is difficult, forgetting can be downright impossible for many of us. How can people be expected to forget the most painful experience of their lives? You must keep the idea of forgiveness and forgetting separate. Forgiveness can come without forgetting. In fact, you'll never forget what happened to you no matter whether or not you stay married or with your partner. Forgiveness is optional.

Obviously, there is a great spiritual aspect to the issue of forgiveness, we all know the saying; "To err is human, to forgive divine." (Alexander Pope (1688 - 1744), from *An Essay on Criticism*). Religious teachings tell us that forgiveness is good for the soul and should be freely offered. That may be well and good, but it's much easier said than done.

In a case such as infidelity the offender wants us to hurry up and forgive and forget so they can "put it behind them." But often they fail to give us the basis needed to forgive. Often, they don't come clean and tell us everything. Sometimes, they fail to even make a heartfelt apology or show regret. Then too, they don't recognize the importance of repayment. The following quote from Willard F. Harley, Jr., Ph.D. author of the book, *His Needs Her Needs: Building An Affair Proof Marriage* clearly describes the concept.(His website, marriagebuilders.com is one of the best)

"First let's try to understand what forgiveness is. One illustration is telling a person who owes you $10,000 that he won't have to pay you back. You "forgive" the debt. In other words, forgiveness is eliminating an obligation of some sort.

But we generally don't think of money when we think of the need of forgiveness. Instead, we are concerned about inconsiderate behavior that has caused us great pain and suffering -- the pain that an affair causes, for example. Forgiveness in these situations means thinking about the person as if the offense never took place. That is extremely difficult to do. The offended spouse usually thinks *what he or she can do to make it up to me. How can I be compensated for the pain I've suffered?*"

To make matters worse, whenever a wayward spouse sees me for counseling there is rarely regret and rarely a willingness to compensate the offended spouse. They usually ask to be forgiven, but that doesn't mean he or she is deeply remorseful. It usually means that he or she doesn't want us to bring up the subject anymore, or require a change in behavior. In other words, the wayward spouse wants the pain suffered by the offended spouse to be ignored or forgotten. Like a $10,000 debt, they want it forgiven, and then they want to borrow another $10,000.

I'm in favor of forgiveness in many situations, but this isn't one of them. In the case of infidelity, compensation not only helps the offended spouse overcome the resentment he or she harbors, but the right kind of compensation helps restore the relationship and prevents the painful act from being repeated."

Discussion question:

So, if that is the case, what would be just compensation to you for your spouse's affair?

What if you are divorced and don't have a snowball's chance in a pizza oven of ever getting so much as *unjust* compensation? Are we going to face life harboring an un-forgiven burden and the pain of the betrayal? What do we do then? Again, we can turn to spiritual guidance and find that the idea of forgiveness is "good for the soul" or following in the footsteps of God. But, is it really good for the soul and how do we move from being human with human frailties to superhuman?

According to the website, forgiving.org,

> "Research and personal observations show that the person who forgives is happier and healthier. While the goal of forgiving may be noble, the effects are concrete."

Richard Fitzgibbons cites these benefits to the one who forgives:

- Decreased levels of anger and hostility;
- Increased feelings of love;
- Improved ability to control anger;
- Enhanced capacity to trust;
- Freedom from the control of events of the past;
- No longer repeating negative behaviors;
- Improved physical health;
- Significant improvement in psychiatric disorders; "

That is quite an impressive list of benefits, and don't forget the idea of cleansing of the soul, it is considered a benefit by most people and experts. In fact, some researchers say that forgiveness has more benefits for the forgiver than the forgiven. I'm personally not totally convinced of that yet, but perhaps one day I will believe. In fact, I believe that it is the other way around. Having forgiven my wife I've not yet seen all those benefits. However, you may find it 100% true so as with all things; do what is right for you.

Questions to consider:

In your own circumstances, can you see any benefits to forgiving, even if your partner has left you or refuses to justly compensate you?

What might be the adverse consequences of forgiving an unrepentant spouse?

What are the consequences to you of not forgiving?

If you are struggling with the very idea of forgiving your partner (or yourself), you are not alone.

> "It takes courage and commitment to act in a more forgiving fashion. It is not at all a sign of weakness but a mark of strength."
> Dr. Carl Thorensen, Stanford University.

> "If I hold a grudge because I'm angry, I feel strong. But to set that anger aside takes real strength."
> Everett L. Worthington, Jr.

In order to forgive, it is important to understand what forgiveness is and is not. I believe that there is a lot of misunderstanding related to forgiveness and a few quotes from famous people may help us sort it out.

Archbishop Desmond Tutu once said: "Forgiveness is taking seriously the awfulness of what has happened when you are treated unfairly. Forgiveness is not pretending that things are other than the way they are." Forgiveness then is not just ignoring what has happened to you.

Dr. Ken Hart, as quoted in *Zest Magazine* (UK), October 2000 said: "Forgiveness does not equal forgetting. It is about healing the memory of the harm, not erasing it."

Your forgiveness does not release a person from paying the price for what they did. Murderers are often forgiven by the victim's family but still go to jail. Forgiveness is also not excusing someone's actions. They are still liable for what they have done.

Forgiveness does not require reconciliation and it does not mean that you will trust your partner again. You can forgive them but it does not mean they need to be a part of your life.

Alan Paton, author of *Cry, the Beloved Country* " said: "When a deep injury is done to us, we never recover until we forgive." In many experts' opinion, forgiveness is necessary to fully recover from an injustice.

Robert D. Enright, PhD. Author of *Forgiveness is a Choice* said: "Forgiving is an act of mercy toward an offender. We are no longer controlled by angry feelings toward this person." If you are inclined to be merciful, forgive your partner. It is however, important to not allow anger to continue to hurt your own health. If forgiving will help you, do it.

Richard Fitzgibbons, author of "*Anger and the Healing Power of Forgiveness: A Psychiatrist's View*" said "Forgiveness works directly on the emotion of anger and related constructs such as resentment, hostility, or hatred by diminishing the intensity or level within the mind and heart."

That is a very good thing. I know from my own experience that anger can eat away at your life and your relationships.

Jimmy Carter, 39th President of the United States said: "I think it means...putting yourself in the position of the other person, and wiping away any sort of resentment and antagonism you feel toward them."

I'm not saying here that all those renowned people are right but in most aspects, what they say seems to make a lot of sense. But now, we reach the $64,000 question. How can you forgive in spite of no remorse, no just compensation and no help at all from the offender?

The keys are to *forgive yourself* and then deal with all of the obstacles that get in the way of forgiveness for your partner. The idea of forgiving yourself is perhaps the most important aspect, it allows you to take back control of your life and move on yourself.

We talked early on about blaming ourselves and that is an element at work here. In essence, we seem to harbor those blames regardless of what we say to ourselves or what good advice we hear (like this book.) You need to surface all those things you blame yourself for (and those your partner has blamed you for) and forgive them in yourself.

Discussion questions:

What are the emotional obstacles to forgiveness? How can you personally overcome them?

Here is an excerpt from *Healing Currents Magazine*, Sept/Oct 1996 on steps to forgiveness by Frederic Luskin, Ph.D.

> "The process of forgiveness can be a liberating experience, one that if practiced proactively can lead to a wonderful experience of life. Interestingly, forgiveness can only occur because we have been given the gift of the ability to make choices. We have the choice to forgive or not to forgive and no one can force us to do either. Conversely, if we want to forgive someone no one can stop us no matter how poorly they may act. This ability to forgive is a manifestation of the personal control we have over our lives. It is nice to reflect upon and feel the respect that we have been given to be able to make such profound choices.
>
> Compellingly, the option to forgive also implies that we had discretion as to whether or not we took offense in the first place. While forgiving may be a difficult enough choice for many of us, imagine how our lives would be if we rarely or never used our power of choice to take

offense. Since we have choice, wouldn't it make sense to limit the amount of times we are hurt or offended so that the need to forgive rarely if ever arises? The ability to live life without taking offense, without giving blame, and by offering forgiveness are choices that offer a life of great peace.

The ability to offer proactive forgiveness proceeds along four steps. At step one you are filled with self justified anger. At some point in your life you have been hurt and you are mad at the person you feel wronged you. You blame the person committing the wrong for how you are feeling. It is their action and not your choice of response that you feel is at the cause of your anger. You have forgotten that you have a choice as to how you will react, or are so angry that you are convinced that it would not be right to forgive the offense. At this stage there is usually both active and submerged anger.

The second step towards forgiveness emerges when after feeling angry with someone for a while you realize that the anger does not feel good to you. It may be hurting your emotional balance or your physical health. Or you wish to repair the damage to the relationship. So you take steps to forgive. You may begin to see the problem from the other person's point of view or you may simply decide to let the problem go. In either case after an extended period of time you are no longer angry and you have forgiven the person with whom you were angry. This process can be applied to anger at oneself, another person or to life in general.

The third stage of forgiveness comes after you have seen the beneficial results of forgiveness and you choose to let go of your anger fairly quickly. In this stage the choice is to feel the hurt for a short period of time, and then work to either repair the relationship or let go of seeing the situation as a problem. In either case you decide to forgive because you have had some practice with it and see the benefit in your life. This could emerge in as simple a situation as being cut off by another car on the expressway or in a complex situation like an affair in a marriage. At this stage you are aware that the length of time you experience the situation as a grievance is primarily up to you.

The fourth stage of forgiveness involves the proactive choice to rarely if ever get angry. This means often to forgive in advance of a specific trigger. This stage often emerges at the same time as some or all of the following thoughts:

I don't want to waste my precious life in the discomfort caused by anger so I will choose to feel differently. I am able to forgive myself, forgive others, forgive life, and forgive God.

I know how it hurts when people don't forgive me. I do not want to hurt other people by my anger so I will let it go.

Life is filled with incredible beauty and I am missing some if I am experiencing unresolved anger. I forgive myself for getting sidetracked.

People do the best they can and if they err I can best help them by offering understanding. The first step in this process is to forgive the specific offense.

Everyone, including myself operates primarily out of self-interest. I must expect that some times I, in my self-interest, will be annoyed by some one else's expression of their self-interest. If I can understand that this is an ordinary part of life, what is there to be upset about? If I understand that self-interest is the way that I behave, how can I but offer forgiveness to everyone, including myself for behaving that way?

These four stages of forgiveness will not be followed in the same way by all people and in all relationships. There are some people for whom we feel such love that we are almost always at stage four: open hearted and ready to forgive. There are other people for whom we feel so egregiously hurt and our well of good will for them is so dry that we can spend years at stage one. What is critical to remember is the power of personal choice and the importance of exercising that choice to forgive so that we can bring peace and healing into our relationships and ourselves."

One more question for you to think about:

How important is it to you to have your *spouse forgive you* for all the things they told you "forced" them into an affair? Or is that even an issue?

If it is an issue, then talk to them about it. Tell them how you feel and that at some point you expect and need them to "forgive" you in some way. That forgiveness could be simply an apology for saying those things and that they really did not mean it or a heartfelt forgiveness if they honestly believe it to be true.

Much has been said about how forgiveness helps a person heal. However, I am one of a few voices in the wilderness who believes that though it does usually have benefits and is often called for, it is not always necessary. I see no value in forgiving someone who has no remorse for what they have done. I see no purpose in forgiving someone who fails to atone for their transgression. I see no reason to forgive someone who continues to hurt you and play games with your life. Regardless of what the experts say, forgiveness truly is divine and I am not. I am human and though I have the power within me to forgive someone who hurts me so deeply and fails to make up for it, I have to make the decision to do so and it has to be right for me.

The experts would no doubt howl their disagreement but I personally believe that forgiveness is more for the one who committed the wrongdoing than the offended and sometimes they just need to marinate in their own stew of offenses. Forgiving my wife (I did) did absolutely nothing to make me feel a bit better about what she did or about myself. I also believe that much of the motivation for forgiving others is founded in religion or faith. In many cases, your religion will teach you it is good for the soul and you should forgive. Do so only and if the person involved has earned it and when it is right for you and only you. Not one minute sooner. I've taken some heat for those ideas from some of my readers, one of whom down rated my book in a review because they disagreed. Regardless, I stand by it as my opinion and if you see no value in forgiving someone and feel comfortable with that decision, more power to you.

Once it is all said and done, you'll find that it is hard to sort out whether you've forgiven them from the fact that you will always remember and have that scar on your soul. When you remember, it often feels like the hurt is still right there in your heart and then sometimes the anger returns. Then you feel as though you've not forgiven them. I'm not sure myself whether we really fully forgive someone who hurts us so much. Perhaps we do, but in a limited way. Some days I feel that I've forgiven my wife and other days I feel otherwise. I think only when we find true inner peace, will forgiveness and remembrance be reconciled.

As for the other person, the "experts" say you should forgive them too. For most of us, that will take longer than forgiving our partner. In my case, I've actually decided I'm not going to forgive the other man, he helped ruin my life and I choose not to forgive him. Perhaps if he had the courage to apologize to me I'd feel differently. Instead he just moved on to someone else's wife. I believe in his case, God, not me should bear the task of forgiveness. In some ways I feel he deserves eternal condemnation. I loved my wife so feel that in her case, it is up to me to forgive her. Believe me; I do not care a whit about the other man so I'll just leave it to someone who cares to do the forgiving. As with all things related to healing after an affair, it just takes a lot of time to resolve this issue.

Dealing with the Betrayer

Whether or not you part company, you'll probably still have some contact with your partner. If you want to rebuild the relationship, you'll have your work cut out for you. The details and process of reconciliation are beyond the scope of this book, I'm just trying to help you through the worst of times. For the long term, get some of the books I've recommended in chapter 19. Regardless, I'd like to offer you a few thoughts on dealing with the offending partner that might help take just a smidgen of tension out of the process.

It's dangerous to offer advice because I've always tried to be non directive with the people in my support group. What is good for me may be poison for you. Only you know the best thing to do in your own situation and only you can make the right decision. I have said this before and it bears repeating. Do not let others make your decisions for you. That said here are some thoughts for you regarding how you possibly can deal with your partner for the short term.

Not knowing at this time for sure whether you will reconcile or part (unless they've already flown the coop), it is important to try to keep yourself under control. Don't be an idiot like me who goes off on wild tantrums that simply makes things worse. Try your best to be logical and dispassionate in your dealings and discussions. If your case ends up in court, you want to be the one who is pure and on the high road. By now you've probably blown that if you are like the rest of us, but get control now.

Don't bait your partner or put yourself in a position of possible violence. Be nice and steady. To the extent possible, act neutrally as though you don't care which way they go. That action will drive them nuts. Read *Love Must Be Tough* or the *Solo Partner* for the details on how this can put you in charge.

Likewise, don't let them bait you into an argument. This is very difficult given your emotional state but it is essential. It will drive them to distraction if you fail to take the bait and eventually you will enjoy watching their head blow up when they are frustrated by your refusal to fall into their traps.

Don't beg and blubber on about how much you need them. This will only push them away. Be careful what you put in writing. This is especially critical if you end up in divorce court. You may find what you have said and done being used against you. You don't need that additional annoyance.

Don't force any issue. If you want to talk about it and they refuse, no manner of yelling and begging will change their stand Just explain your reasons and needs in a calm manner and tell them how you feel about their refusal and drop it. Not forever, but at the moment. Keep trying and don't give up, just don't try to make them do anything they refuse to do, it only makes them stand more firmly and resist.

In case your partner wants to reconcile, you must establish a firm set of rules for them to accept. Those rules have to include NO CONTACT of any kind with their fellow adulterer and a firm and clear end to the affair. One way of doing that is through a letter, email or even a phone call (with you listening.)

In our chapter on building trust, I mentioned we'd address that issue again in this chapter. In dealing with a partner who has betrayed you, it is their actions that truly tell whether the person is really sincere in wanting honesty and trust or just saying it because it seems right. This all has to come from the heart. You may hear them say, "I'm sorry" or "I won't ever do it again," but you know that they probably said that to you before. "Listen" to their actions, not their words.

I mentioned the requirement for "no contact." It is critical that they provide you with assurance from time to time and demonstrate that they are avoiding that person like the plague. You can't take anything on blind faith anymore.

They should go out of their way to show you they are committed to being honest and trustworthy. *This is important, if they balk or hesitate at anything you ask for their cooperation on, it will send an instant unspoken but very strong message that they are still setting boundaries.* Doing so leaves you with the question as to what is beyond that boundary. It makes you feel that they still have secret corners in their life that they want to hide from you. At this point, they will need to forget about personal "space" or privacy or control. Marriage or any committed relationship is not about privacy or secrecy or control. It is about sharing your lives and ministering to each other's needs.

They've got to be proactive in being completely accountable to you. When the cell phone bills come, they should show them to you before you ask. When they read email, they should tell you about it and even print any that are important or ask you to log in at anytime or feel free to sit with them when they do their mail. Without you having to ask, they should make their life an open book. If they act proactively, you will feel they really DO want to be honest.

They will have to take care to never, ever, lie to you again over anything. I'd say never because once trust is gone, any additional deceptions set you back. It's like building a wall of security. All the actions we've mentioned put bricks back into a wall that has been torn down. Honesty and actions are the mortar that binds the bricks. One lie, no matter how small causes the wall to tumble down and you must start all over again. With their lies they've proven they cannot be trusted. They are at zero on the trustworthy scale and have a lot of work to do to rebuild the trust you previously gave them. One slip and it just compounds things.

If your partner hesitates or shows no indication of being open, then their trustworthiness is questionable and that should help you make a decision on whether to stay or not.

It may not suit you to look at their side now but in many respects, the way they are acting towards you is probably tainted by their own defensiveness in having been "found out." Many of us who have discovered our partner's betrayal have experienced their extremely aggressive response. Consider that when they are discovered they are immediately on the defensive. Many people subscribe to the Bill Clinton method of a good offense being the best defense and his corollary rule of "deny, deny, deny." My wife was so defensive she was mean and cruel. Not only that, in the face of printed emails between her and her lover, she accused me of making them up!

I know you are probably not in a mood to be very sympathetic towards them but realize that much of their reaction is a natural one when a person is cornered or caught doing something wrong. Take that into consideration and try to understand (not sympathize) that they are human too and the reaction is not something unexpected. It's far too late to deal with initial reactions but it isn't too late to more or less disregard all that transpired on the day of discovery and the period immediately after. Don't bring it all up again and again as it will do nothing to improve things and allow you to move forward with recovery (and them too.)

Something else to consider is that except in the most grievous cases of self indulgence and disregard for others, most adulterers reach a point at which they realize that what they did was wrong.

At that point they will begin to feel remorse and be sorry for what they did. It may take them a while to communicate that to you but I think all but the most dedicated "players" reach that point fairly soon. Of course at first, they'll be mostly sorry for getting caught but later the enormity of their mistake will become self evident. So you may say, "so what, so they feel bad, tough!" That is also not an unexpected reaction but you should stop and think before you reject it. If you hope to reconcile or reach the level of a decent relationship with this person ever again, you must realize that they too are human and like all of us, do things they regret. I'll bet you've got something in your past you'd rather not remember or are not proud of too. Logically you should recognize this and at some point, cut them some slack for being human.

As hard as it may be right now, have some pity and try to understand their reactions to your discovery and that they are human and will most likely ultimately regret everything they have done to you. Believe it or not, they might even realize that it was not your fault and that you were not as bad a person as they said you were to justify their actions. Don't force the issue, it will come about in good time so keep the faith and show some understanding when it does seem that they are coming around.

The Other Person (OP)

When I first wrote this book my focus on the other person, we call them the "OP," was essentially non-existent except for portraying them as a demon who wrecked our life. Though I've made some reference to them in various chapters, mostly I've ignored them and their role. Over the years I've collected a few observations and want to share them with you with a major focus being on how you react to them and potentially interact with them.

My first thought and suggestion to you is to *not* interact with them unless there is some compelling issue or requirement to do so. Most of us harbor a great deal of resentment and anger towards the OP and usually, interaction with them becomes an ugly confrontation. For that reason, my primary thought is for you to simply leave them alone. Your focus should not be on them it should be on your own recovery and that of your relationship if that is the direction you've chosen.

Among the reasons for meeting them is the possibility of revenge. I discussed this elsewhere mostly in the context of revenge against your partner. It is very important that you also try your best to avoid acts of revenge against the OP. I know how hard that can be. For years, I've wanted to somehow harm the OP and I've heard so many others like you and I who have said the same. But, it's just not always the smartest thing to do.

For one thing, your revenge could backfire depending on just how far you take it. If you do something that can be construed as harassment, physical vandalism to property or even physical harm to the OP, you are going to be the one who pays the price. Sometimes that price could be jail time and legal bills that can ruin you financially.

In the heat of anger, I've heard some say it would be worth it. At one time I felt the same way. Locked in a prison of pain and anguish over a partner's affair, being isolated in a cell, away from it all can actually seem attractive. However, we know that once the fog and anger clears, spending a few months or years in jail is not a great idea. So hold off on revenge till you see clearly and can think through the consequences.

Many of us who have been betrayed have some kind of compulsion to meet with the person, especially if we know nothing of them or have never seen them. There is some sort of morbid curiosity that seems to come out. Part of it is comparative thinking. I see this thinking mostly in women who want to see "the bitch" to compare their beauty and physical attractiveness to themselves. To this I also say, don't bother. I can tell you that most cases of adultery do not involve some gorgeous top model who is a knock down drag out hottie. Men don't seem as interested in seeing the other guy. I think that is because our male ego is so fragile and we would rather not know than run the risk of seeing that our wife chose some hulking hunk hung like a mule.

Almost all of us who have been betrayed by infidelity discover that the OP is nothing special. In fact the most common description I've heard from women about the OP is that "she is a dog." Same with men, the OP is most often unremarkable in the looks department. Often this comes as a shock. Why on earth would someone have an affair with someone no more attractive than us? Another common question is "what the heck did they see in her (him) that I don't have?" The answer to that lies in the fact that affairs are most often not about physical attractions as much as they are about emotional attractions. Sure, physical attraction can play a part in it but affairs usually happen due to some emotional connection that develops over time into a sexual one.

Some women I know have established a rather strange relationship with the OW (other woman) that borders on friendship. I remember one woman who showed up at one of our support group meetings with a friend whom she said also had been betrayed by an affair. Of course we took her in with open arms and offered all of our support. Well, near the end of the meeting the new person confessed that her betrayal was by the husband of the woman who brought her in that she had an affair with him and felt he betrayed her by lying and cheating on *her with his own wife!* After meeting her, the wife realized (rightfully) that they had both been betrayed by the same man. Surely in different ways but betrayed by him just the same. They then became bonded by their hatred for him. This adds some real meaning to the idea that adversity makes for strange bedfellows.

We were totally shocked by that revelation and unfortunately, we had to inform her that she (the OW) could no longer attend since the group was for those who had been betrayed by a spouse's affair, not one who had the affair. Having an OP in the meetings makes for a very uncomfortable situation for many of us and inhibits our own healing so she simply had to go. As a postscript to that, the wife went ballistic on us and was quite defensive of the OW and very angry with us for evicting her new found friend. Of course she never returned either.

There is a lesson there about the OP that perhaps at this time you are not interested in hearing, but you know I'm going to share it with you anyway. That lesson is that in many cases, the OP is a human being too and sometimes they are deeply hurt and scarred by the affair. Though most of us have little pity for someone who gets involved with someone who is married or committed to another, we've learned that affairs are usually not something people plan, they often just happen through initial attractions that escalate over time.

Yes, there are exceptions. Some people, mostly guys, are professional sexual predators. The guy who took my wife has had multiple affairs; he is a true player who just loves to screw other men's wives. Perhaps the woman or man who had an affair with your special someone was the same, it happens. But, in the whole, most people on either side of the affair do not set out to have an affair and are often just like you and me.

As hard as it is to contemplate, many of the OPs are deeply hurt by an affair. Sometimes they make such a strong emotional bind that they build up hopes of a new life. Those hopes are most often destroyed just as ours were and they too face a period of loss and emotional devastation that is very upsetting. Perhaps more important to you, they are almost always very, very remorseful about what they did and realize it was a terrible and stupid mistake.

In a very few cases, some people have met with the OP and like the aforementioned case, they have made a bond of sorts. In those cases they have discovered what I've already told you, the OP is often a "normal" person who deeply regrets what happened and who wants to apologize for the hurt it has caused. Sometimes the results of those meetings help eliminate the anger and resolve unanswered questions about why and what was the role of the OP. In those cases it may be beneficial. I must say however that those positive outcomes are not the norm and meetings with the OP more often result in simply making things worse.

Earlier I mentioned that sometimes there is good reason to meet with or somehow connect with the OP. There are few but still there are times it becomes necessary. The biggest reason and one that can cause inestimable additional pain is if the liaison resulted in a pregnancy and child. In that case, one must balance the well being of the child and the father (or mother's) role in the child's future. We've had more than one such case pass through our group and it is gut wrenching to see the additional pain and hard decisions a betrayed spouse must deal with in such a case. If this is the case for you, my heart goes out to you.

One of our long term members of our support group grappled with this issue for years. She felt that her husband should be a part of the child's life so made every attempt to take the child in as her own and love him and allow her husband to continue to see the mother (OW). Her actions were as caring and unselfish as any I've seen. Her deep faith allowed her to cope but it was still apparent that seeing the OW with her husband or knowing they were together with the child was like a knife through the heart every time. Such personal sacrifice is rare and worth noting. Unfortunately, in the end, her husband continued to have a closer relationship with the OW than was necessary and after years of struggle, the marriage finally was dissolved.

The one thing I've always hoped for was one special contact from "him" but it has never come. That would be a simple apology for destroying my marriage and life for several years. Perhaps you've hoped the same. Unfortunately, that day never comes, for many reasons. Either they really could care less or they are too embarrassed, too remorseful and simply cannot face you. If you are waiting for this to happen, let it go as you'll probably never see that day come.

Regardless of the exceptions, remember that they are just exceptions and that for the most part, contact with the OP can and more often does result in unnecessary additional pain, anguish and sometimes legal consequences. This may be the only place in the book where I give that lousy, laughable and almost impossible advice that those who don't understand give us; get past it, move on. Think it through when you can and write down the perceived advantages of contact and the probable negative consequences. I think you'll find that it most likely is a losing proposition for you and you should just "fagettaboutit."

For The One
Who Had the Affair

Though this book is clearly for the person who has been hurt by the affair, the person who has had the affair can play a huge part in whether or not we recover and how soon. To that end, this chapter is written especially for the person who had the affair. I've added it to this expanded edition for those who have had an affair and are already committed to rebuilding their relationship or for those who are on the fence. If that is the case, if you think it will help ask them to read it. But first you read it and decide if it will help.

So you had an affair and now you are going through the aftermath. If you have already made up your mind that none of this is your fault and you have no intention of changing, then don't waste your time by reading any more. If however, you really understand that what has happened is a result of bad choices you made and want to "make up" for it and restore your relationship, please do read on.

You should be prepared that some, maybe all of what I say to you may make you angry. If so, please don't let that stop you from looking for the truth in what I say. You have to confront some pretty ugly truths about yourself to get beyond where things are today and in many cases I'm going to be the bad guy who makes you look in the mirror and see what you need to see and change about your current situation. As ugly as it may be, if you really want to make things better, you've got to look harshly at your own actions, attitudes and behavior.

I think the first thing you should consider is just how utterly devastating what you did has been to those who love you and placed their trust in you. It may be hard for you to understand and I honestly know that you'd rather not contemplate it, but give it some serious thought. It might even help you to read the first few chapters of this book to get an idea of just how deep the pain goes.

Often, when a person has an affair, and is caught, the last thing they want to do is dwell on it. I know that you would much rather put it behind you and move on but it's important that you understand that it is not that easy for us. In your case, it is a chapter you'd like to put behind you. After all, who wants to be reminded day in and day out what a jerk they were? You'll just have to face up to it because though you can stash it away and move on, you must be prepared for a very long road to recovery for the person you betrayed. That means your own discomfort will be extended way beyond what you'd like. The good news is that you can do so much to help your partner recover and in doing so, you can significantly shorten the process. Please recognize that though the affair may have been about you and your needs, it's not about you anymore. It is now about your committed relationship and helping your partner survive this awful devastation.

The first thing you must do is realize that you made some really bad choices and you had so many other options to avoid this. The natural tendency when you are caught in an affair is to immediately blame your spouse. If you did read other parts of this book, you saw that blaming them is absurd and a defense mechanism on your part. Drop the defenses, admit you were wrong and focus on recovery not blame.

Of course you may really think it is their fault and maybe there were things they did that you think justify what you did. Sorry, there is no real justification for such betrayal and dishonesty. You could have been honest and openly confronted the issues in a constructive way. You could have told us that you were attracted to someone. Remember, you've also hurt the person with whom you had the affair so you also have betrayed them (see the previous chapter). You could have lived up to your marriage vows and been honest with the other person and said no. It all boils down to honesty. You missed your opportunity before, now it is essential that you not blow it again.

Honesty is going to be the foundation on which a better future can be built. You are probably ashamed of all the lies and things you did behind your partner's back; I hope you are because that is a good start. But now is the time when you can truly make up for it and help both of you face a positive future.

Are you getting angry with this? Go ahead, there is a lot of anger we both face. Your partner is angry that you betrayed them and hurt them. Maybe you are angry because you got caught, or because you feel you were justified. It does not matter. Just as we (the betrayed) have to deal with and eliminate our anger over what happened, you need to do the same. Once we establish honesty as a requisite for the future, we must next make sure that we do not act in anger as we work though this mess.

You cannot rationally improve things if you approach it in anger. I understand that flare-ups will happen; we are all human in that regard. Those times will pass. What I'm referring to is the under the surface constant anger that just erodes away your life and prevents you from working towards an improved situation. So, my advice is to get rid of that chip on your shoulder and start acting like an adult.

You may be wondering, "what's the big deal?" after all, it really meant nothing to me so my spouse should just get over it and understand that I still love them (assuming you do). A recent movie, **Shattered** (2007 starring Pierce Brosnan) has a classic line that may make you understand what the big deal is. In the final scene, after the husband has admitted to an affair (after being caught of course) he says to his wife, "hey, it meant nothing to me." His wife sums up the difference in viewpoints between "us" and "you." She says very quietly, "I know it meant nothing to you but *it meant everything* to me."

It may be very difficult to put yourselves in our shoes but try to understand that what you have done is the most devastating thing that you could ever do to your partner. Imagine if you can that the tables were turned. That some other man was screwing your wife (or woman screwing your husband) and she was having oral sex (you can count on it). She/he then comes home and kisses you hello. How would that go down with you? How many times did you do just that? Disgusting isn't it? How would you feel if you devoted your life to making someone happy (granted you may not think we did try, but just imagine for a moment that we did) and they lived a secret life with someone else? How would you feel if every day you trusted the person you love and found that they had been lying and deceiving you for months or even years?

Empathy; now is the time for all the empathy you can muster and all the patience you can find to help your wounded partner heal. Anything less will cause even more pain. Maybe you don't want to do that, fine, then say so and walk away. If you do feel responsible and do want to repair things, you'll have to do all you can to "make up" for what you have done.

Think about this. You had your fun, your excitement, your "new" sex, your surge of hormones and all the stimulation of the adulterous relationship. In the meanwhile, your spouse was miserable knowing that something was wrong. She or he spent countless hours worrying where you were and what you were doing when you called to tell you had to "work late," had "an important meeting," or were going out with the guys (or girls). I guarantee you that your spouse suspected things. We knew darn well that you were lying. Maybe they even said something and you denied any wrongdoing and gave them a story. I also guarantee that no matter how hard you tried to cover things up, the way you behaved towards them was different than before. You were colder, less interested, avoided sex, argued more and there was more tension because you were stressed while trying to manage two lives. For that reason, is it asking too much for you to be patient and tolerate our anger and emotional imbalance for a few months or even a few years? Again, if you think it is too much to ask, then say so and walk out now because things will never get better if you are so selfish as to not make an effort to give some love back and help us through this.

So, what is it you need to do? I hope you truly want to know. Of course I will tell you but you need to know now it is going to be tough but with some courage and effort you can regain your relationship and hopefully move on (as you want to do) to a much improved situation.

1. If you have not already, you need to absolutely crush the affair forever. If you are hanging on to contact with the other person, you can bet that you'll end up going back to them when the going gets tough. Purge them from your life and let them know in no uncertain terms that you want no further contact either as friend, lover or foe. If you have already done this, good for you. If not, you must do so right now. Put this book down now and either write them an email, letter or call them (with your spouse present) and make sure they clearly understand it is O-V-E-R. You need not be mean to them, as much as I

grudgingly hate to admit, I realize that person meant something to you and know you probably do not want to hurt them any more than you already have. So be diplomatic but firm. Not mean, not vindictive but firm in a manner that leaves no doubt. Then never, ever contact them again.

2. Honesty must rule in everything you do. Rebuilding trust will be the most difficult and lengthy part of recovery so honesty must be constant and unerring. One lie and all you may have done to rebuild trust resets you to zero. They trusted you before out of love and respect, you destroyed that so you have no credibility or trust right now. Any further dishonesty, even a little white lie, will work against you. Though I say this is difficult, ask why it should be? Honesty has to be the underpinning of any relationship and if you love someone, the truth should come easy. Unfortunately, in our society today, it seems the exception.

3. Your life must be an open book. You cannot hide anything from your partner. Nothing. You should be very proactive in this regard. The more proactive you are, the better things will be and the more trust you will build. Withhold things and your partner will be suspicious. This means you share ALL email accounts you have, including passwords. By the way, in today's environment, email is one of the more favored "secret" ways to carry on an illicit affair. It also happens to be the most common avenue of discovery of proof. So don't think you are too clever for someone to find you out. I've seen some pretty clever ways to hack a computer to get proof of adultery and

for every way you can think of to hide it, someone can find it.

4. As a part of the "open book" process you should also share voicemail accounts and passwords. By now you are thinking "what about my privacy?" Let me ask you what it is you feel you need to keep private from your spouse? I honestly believe if you are worried about your privacy then you have something to hide that you shouldn't. If you are serious about rebuilding, you have to accept that in marriage there is no such thing as privacy and if you maintain that there is you will set yourself up for another affair.

5. Continuing with full disclosure, all cell phone bills should be given to your spouse, all credit card bills all other evidence that will support your honesty must be offered. You cannot take the stand that they should ask. Proactively sharing these items with your spouse will assure them that all is well. Again, don't think you can hide "secret" accounts forever either. Sooner or later those will be discovered too. So every month, without fail, hand the bills to them before they ask and/or make sure they see them if they are online.

6. Don't think you are smarter than your spouse. You did get caught didn't you? If you confessed before getting caught, my hat is off to you as you are one of a very few whose conscience finally made them do the right thing. If you were caught, learn a lesson from this and be assured that the vast majority if not all affairs are eventually discovered. It will happen through email, phone records, phone calls, friends, investigators and sometimes even people you confide in will have the courage to tell your spouse because

they know it is wrong to aid in your deception. Don't try to "snow" your spouse ever again. You might get away with it in the short term but not in the long run. Also remember that though you think you are original and clever in covering your tracks, the same tricks have been used for a thousand years and they don't work today any better than they did then. Your ideas may seem new and clever to you but I guarantee, it's all been done before and there are plenty of sources out there for your partner to uncover your deceptions. Don't ever do this again.

7. If you think you might be headed to another affair be fair this time and be honest. Tell your partner you are attracted to someone and tell them why. If you are unhappy with some aspect of your relationship rather than hiding it and seeking to fill a perceived void with someone else, tell your partner. And don't be obtuse, make sure they understand with clarity what the issue is and how you feel. The same advice about being decent in how you present things applies here as it did in dealing with your ex lover.

8. Never, ever blame your partner for what happened. Don't give them a litany of the things you hate about them that drove you to an affair. Don't ever say or imply that they made you do it. This is absurd and destructive. You know as well as I do that much of that is simply rationalization to make you feel better about what you did. If you start the blame game, things will not improve. You and only you were responsible for allowing the affair to happen and the sooner you accept that the better.

9. Show your concern for how things are going by asking your partner how they are doing; ask them if

they are feeling better, worse or the same. Ask what can be done to help make things better. One major problem in just about all relationships is the lack of open discussion about needs that one or both partners have that are not being met. The only way to know what is needed is to ask and for us to respond when asked. This is where your partner needs to be open and honest and help you help them.

10. Be prepared to answer lots of questions about what happened. We need to understand what happened and get answers. It will be very uncomfortable for you to relive some of the aspects of the affair and you may feel compelled to not answer our questions. Being evasive or not fully answering questions will only delay trust. It is common to say "I forgot" when asked uncomfortable questions but you and I both know you have not forgotten. The affair was so exciting that you probably remember every detail. We know that and the only way you could forget is out of convenience. Also, don't be dishonest because you think somehow it will protect us from painful details. Again, being deceptive or evasive will only magnify our need to know and prolong this process. Be open, be honest and get it over with.

I know that this part can be frustrating. If things get to be too much or you feel the questioning is constant, set up a process where you both can cope. I suggest setting aside a period once a day for questions for both of you. At least a half hour up to a maximum of an hour where the two of you can sit down and discuss questions. Then when the time is up, both of you get to give it a rest. If you both agree you don't need or want the time on a given day, then skip it till the next day. This can take a great deal of stress out of your days and allow for a predictable and controlled process.

11. Don't force anything. If you want sex but your partner is not ready, just be patient. If you want them to act happy and they are not, don't expect miracles, it will come in time. Likewise, we should also not force things. This entire process requires patience on both sides and concern for each other.

12. Take time to enjoy each other's company in settings that are fun and even romantic. All the tension requires breaks and so a movie, dinner, concert or picnic can allow you to both have a good time and get to know each other again. The romance part will be a little more difficult and as with many things, be patient. We find it hard to get close again so the burden will mostly be yours to show affection and a little romance.

It is now important to understand that what you did has changed your relationship forever. Where it goes from here will be dependent on how the two of you work together. What will come should be a loving and caring, honest relationship that is different from the one you had before. If you are hoping to have things be as they were, forget that because you now have a different relationship. You may be able to recapture the love you had for each other but remember, "the way we were" was then and this is now. Both of you must understand that what you had is gone and what you will have will be different. Some people say it can be better than what you had and others believe it won't be. This much I will say; it will be different and it can be good. Many aspects will be better. Hopefully among the better things will be honesty. I wish you all the success in the world and know that one day, this chapter in your life can be closed and you will have learned some important lessons about life and love. Finally, I want to offer you the same suggestion I have given your partner. There is a new book out by Peggy Vaughan titled *Preventing Affairs*. In that book you can learn all that it takes to prevent a recurrence and to establish a relationship that will be nearly affair proof. After all, is that not what you had hoped for on your wedding day and promised through your wedding vows? Of course it was and right now it is not too late to live up to your promise at the altar. Details of the book can be found on page 188 in the chapter about the best books. I strongly suggest you and your partner work through the book together.

My Story

You know a little about my personal story from my use of examples and passages from my personal journal. Not that I think my story is unique or even interesting, but I thought that some of my readers might simply be curious as to my story and what lead me to write this book. This chapter will appease that curiosity. I've also included some final thoughts, an afterward, that hopefully will appropriately end this portion of the book.

In the 1970's after a string of unsuccessful and unfulfilling relationships, I met my wife. It was one of those moments that are fabled and told of in romance novels. She simply stopped me in my tracks. We exchanged a look that I know cemented our future together and in a flash, I knew that she was the one for me. Of course I don't think I shared that with her at first but it was there from the beginning. We became friends and one night, out with the folks at work we danced and there was the first kiss. I still remember that electric moment and it will always be the defining moment in my love life.

After that first kiss there was a quiet time where we developed a friendship and trust in each other. Years later, at the urging of her boss at the time, we tried a first date and were one from that moment on. We held off on marriage and sex for a long time but it was inevitable. We fell deeply in love and planned what we called "our miracles." There were several; getting married, having children and growing old together. We were married in 1985, a happy day for both of us and at that point one of our miracles came true.

We had a fun and happy life for about five years and then things started to fall apart. We started a business and then I was transferred out of the country and my wife had to run the business and so we were apart for a year. After we decided to liquidate the company, she joined me and we had a wonderful time for two more years. Yet, there were signs of trouble. She kept our finances to herself, hid bills from me and before I knew it, we were in deep trouble. For the next few years we played a game of hide the money and eventually, we lost everything due to her spending and irresponsibility with money. Twice our house was foreclosed and twice we barely saved it, in one case only a few days before a sheriff's sale.

Of course those days were difficult and I would scream at her, she would promise to do better and then would not. I lost all respect for her and she continued to disrespect me. It was agony. We still seemed to love each other but our life was full of anger and tension. Instead of improving, she got worse and worse. Several times I found boxes of bills that were unpaid and payments that were never mailed.

About six years ago, she had a medical scare and had to have a hysterectomy. I believe that was the beginning of the end for her. The second miracle had never taken place and now there was no hope for it. She wanted so badly to be a mother and now she never could. It devastated her and though she acted like it was no big deal, I knew it was.

For the next three years she became more distant and quite mean spirited. Over time I knew that she was involved with someone else but could not prove it. She'd get phone calls from men she worked with and always tell me it was work related and that they were "just friends." After her surgery she lost a lot of weight and started dressing differently. Well, you know exactly the feeling and you know what happened next. Like you, I knew she was involved with someone but could not get the proof. They always seem to go out of their way to look good for their lover but not us.

Three years ago we went on a cruise and she said, it was a "chance to make things better." Little did I know that she was already screwing her asshole work buddy and spent the entire cruise calling him, emailing him and telling him how much she missed him (I'll tell you in a minute how I discovered this). She was telling him what a terrible person I was and all the things that help rationalize their actions. How is it that a person can lie to your face, tell you they love you and that they want to make things better and then run to their lover and screw their brains out? It is nothing short of evil.

After the cruise, as you'd expect, things were not better, in fact they continued to get worse. Sex was a joke. She would turn her head away from me and lay there like a two bit whore all the while no doubt wishing she was fucking her friend. Sometimes she would get angry when I asked for sex and would turn her head and just give me a very unsatisfying hand job. It was so painful; it hurts to think about it even now. We'd argue constantly about finances and sex. She'd tell me I wanted it too much and I'd say she had no sex drive. She once said very indignantly, "there is nothing wrong with my sex drive." Of course later I would know why she said that, she had plenty of drive and she was fucking herself to death with her "just friend."

One day I just had a hunch and decided to check her email. Nothing there; I thought, well, maybe she left stuff in her out basket. That's the moment, my world collapsed. Appropriately, April fools day, 2004. I found a year's worth of emails between them in that folder talking about how much they wanted to fuck. She told him over and over what a negative person I was and how she could not wait to spread her legs for him. I found page after page of descriptions of what they had been doing and what they had planned. It was an unbelievably graphic and painful X rated history of their affair. She said things to him she'd never said to me. She was sexually aggressive in ways she had never been with me. I felt cheated. This man took my wife and played her like a violin and she loved every minute of it. All the while smiling at me and lying her ass off.

I confronted her. I read from the emails, she denied it. I showed her the printouts; unbelievably she tried to say that I had made them up and asked "where did you get those." It amazes and infuriates me how incredibly stupid they must think we are. I was so angry I shouted and cried and she just acted so cold. She finally admitted it and of course continued to lie about the extent of the affair, even when presented with proof.

You read in earlier chapters a bit about my reaction, I went to kill the bastard, sat in front of his house and then left to go see a counselor. He of course told me to leave her. I packed an overnight bag and got in the car and just started driving. I was so in pain and could hardly see the road for my tears. I drove and drove and wished to die. She would call me and tell me to come home and I'd yell at her called her a whore, a bitch, a miserable cock sucker and every other name in the book. I wanted to die and I wanted to live. I thought about driving into a bridge, chickened out. I thought about just getting out of the car and walking into the woods and hoping a bear would kill me. That is laughable now but that is exactly how I was thinking. I cried and cried and cried.

I stopped at a small town a hundred miles or so away, got a hotel room and bought a fifth of rum. I drank myself sick. I was so drunk I could not stand up, I had to crawl to the bathroom to throw up and I did, several times. I called her and screamed at her, I cried, I sent a goodbye email from my laptop and eventually passed out on the floor.

The next day I drove home and thus began a very long and painful period of trying to mend things. My own dreams were dashed forever and I hated her for what she had done. We talked of divorce and separation but it did not happen. I know she stayed in touch with him for a long while afterward and was probably fucking him in the back seat of the car for a long time after D day. I found that she had been buying car parts for him. I found that they had skipped work and rented hotel rooms. They usually fucked in the back seat of the car and even did it in my house while I was away. The indignity of it all is so crushing.

I read voraciously and asked her to. She refused for the most part to read much but finally read Peggy Vaughan's book *The Monogamy Myth*, and it seemed to open her eyes a little.

For the longest time she refused to talk to me and tell me what happened. We both went to counseling and both ended up on drugs to calm us and take away the depression. She was so uncooperative that I finally decided that was it and told her one day that it was over, I wanted a divorce. She was quiet for a few days and then said that she wanted to try to work it out. That was 18 months ago and we are still struggling. (That was said at the time of the first writing of this book. By now, four years later there is less to no struggle)

I know that she was still staying in touch with him up for a long time. A few months back she started to apologize and told me she was going to make it up to me. In many respects she has. She's made a tremendous effort to change and has shown me a great deal of love and what seems to be honest contrition. Her counseling has helped and we've begun to recover.

It's not easy and if you decide to reconcile, get ready for a long and painful road. I still have serious trouble believing her. She lied to me for 15 years and it's hard to overcome that. Day by day I am more trusting and day by day things seem better. But, there are relapses and I'm very afraid. I'm afraid that she might do it again. I don't think I can take that. She says never but I always think, "You've said that before." You too will deal with these sorts of feelings.

I suppose I'll never feel the same about her. The woman I loved and married is now someone else. I've had to give up on that person and am learning to accept and love this new person. Everything has changed and, that is something you must learn to accept as well. Things will never be the same, the person you thought you were in love with is someone else now and you'll have to give it up forever. Things can never be restored to the state they were before the affair. All my dreams are gone, replaced by nothing like them. All I have now is a desire to live life and find some joy of life again. Sometimes I used to think that would never happen but I didn't give up, and neither should you. Though we were both discouraged by the fact that our second miracle (a child) never happened, in retrospect I feel it was God's wisdom. I would have hated to go through this with children. If you are, my heart goes out to you as it seriously complicates recovery and your children will be affected for the rest of their life.

Not long after discovering her affair, I was searching for help and ran across Peggy Vaughan's Beyond Affairs Network of support groups. You can find it now at beyondaffairs.com. I needed contact with others and some support from people that would understand. There was no group in my area so I volunteered to form one. I have many years experience as a professional trainer and management facilitator so thought my skills may be useful. I managed to get a group going and thus far have helped well over 150 people find sanity and comfort. The involvement in the BAN group allowed me to shift my focus from myself to helping others and in the course of doing so, noticed that there were some real issues that those of us who have been betrayed need immediate help with. I wrote a series of "discussion guides" for the group that looked at various aspects of healing and published them. Those guides became the core chapters of this book.

As my group grew, each week we would get new members and it seemed we were always resetting to zero to help the new people. In trying to find a way to help newly betrayed people, I decided that compiling those guides into one volume along with some words of comfort learned along the way might be a way to help people get "up to speed" in the healing process. That is what ultimately lead to this book. My wife has been exceptionally supportive in my efforts to coordinate the support group as well as write this book. In a turn of fortunes, she has been my strength and encouragement that has helped it to become a reality.

Sometimes I wanted to give up and so will you. Your story is probably different with different complications but I assure you, so many of the feelings and challenges you face have been faced by me and many other people. Take comfort in knowing we understand and that we have survived and overcome this terrible burden.

It has been over four years now since the discovery of the affair and I can assure you that things are much improved. My wife has continued to try to be honest and loving and my pain has faded to something that is more a memory than a current issue. Though from time to time I do have flashbacks, they are usually gone as soon as they come and the obsessive thoughts rarely come at all. From time to time I have panic attacks and periods of worry but I can live my life without the terrible constant millstone around my neck and find enjoyment in being together. Of course the relationship is different and I've had to accept my wife for who she is now, not who she was. I do lament the loss of what we had (or what I thought we had) but am mostly satisfied with the way things are today. The fog is gone and I can function without emotional pain. Sure, occasionally a movie or something will momentarily upset me, maybe even make me cry but like all things, that is a rarity. You too can look forward to better times.

If reconciliation is achieved or desired, once you have done so and both of you have reached some equilibrium, it should go without saying that preventing future affairs should be your number one objective as a couple. Until recently there was no guidance on this subject but recently (May, 2008) Peggy Vaughan published the first and only book of its kind that provides a solid roadmap for establishing a marriage that will last and minimize the possibility of an affair. As soon as you are able to focus on the future, I urge you to immediately get a copy of her new book *Preventing Affairs* and both of you work through it together. The book is based on the first reliable research into the subject and offers the very best expert guidance to have an affair free relationship. You can find out more about the book and its availability at: www.preventingaffairs.com.

My final thoughts to you are that you will survive. This hell will end and you'll find happiness again. It will be tough but please don't give up. I pray that your time to heal will be short and that you will have found some help and comfort through this book. I'll pray for you and every other person like "us" who has been so broken. Whether you believe in God, Jesus or the Great Spirit in the sky, spirituality can help. Some days I'd cry out to God to help me and he did, I'm here, I'm alive and I'm finding a new way. So too will you. God bless you and keep you in your journey.

Thoughts from Those Who Have Been There

One of the greatest comforts for those of us facing the devastation of an affair can be the support and thoughts of those who have gone before us. Others who have walked in your shoes can understand what you are going through as no one else can. The value of support of others cannot be underestimated. The Beyond Affairs Network of support groups has been a life ring that has saved many of us from drowning in our own sorrows and pain. For over four years, I have been involved in BAN and can honestly say that without it and the support of the over 150 people I've met through it, I would have taken much longer to recover, if at all.

From those people I have learned many things and in this chapter, I want to share with you some of the wisdom and thoughts that my friends in our support group have shared with me. I hope that by reading these comments, you will be reassured that things will be better and you will survive. I know that sometimes it seems that you will not, but the testimony of thousands such as you and I say otherwise and through their words, I hope you can find hope for your own future and see that you are not alone.

These quotes are edited only for clarity and to eliminate names and possible identities of the writers. Only the month and year of the statement is included to identify separate thoughts from different people.

"I can square up to this bitter cup and lay hold of it with both hands. I can take a point of destructive behavior and make it a point of reference from which I will plot a new course. I may not know which way to go or how to even begin, but I can look for help because I see things differently now. I will learn from each failure so that I will not be the same person I am today. I will accept my responsibility and I will learn to stand strong when others try dragging me back to that pool of misery. I will find those exceptional few that will support me to walk, run and sometimes crawl an exceptional path. I will not tolerate just surviving; I will live, I will thrive and by Grace, I will overcome. If I am courageous, this will be my choice, I've made my choice. What's yours?" (September, 2004)

"I can't give you any answers but I can tell you I understand what you are going through. When someone stays in a marriage it is not the unoffending spouses fault. I have found though that all of the offenders tend to blame the victim." (December, 2004)

"Internalizing what you've discovered will be difficult. One thing is for sure, YOU are not a bad person." (August, 2004)
"Do not let him get the best of you! I will share with you what a friend of mine once said to her husband. She had cancer and was going through chemo and fought time and time again and he just kept putting off the divorce......She said, Look, if you are waiting for me to die, you have a long wait! I am not going anywhere, so you might as well give me a divorce and go on with your life, because that is the only way you will get rid of me! I just laughed and thought what great encouragement that statement was and how much difference pure determination makes in our life. If we think something is impossible it will be, if we think we can't make it through something, we won't." (February, 2005)

"I know how you feel; I've been there with those sorts of feelings and still have them from time to time. The good news is that the anger will abate and you'll begin to move ahead and life will be good again. For sure, you'll always remember what he did and how it hurt you but more on an intellectual level. So say all those who have gone before us. In general, the timetable seems to be 2 years but each day gets better than the last and you can begin to function again.

It's easy to say "put it behind you" but we know that it is not so easy to do so. Try not to let your anger define your future or even your today." (February 2005)

"Here are some things to bear in mind and perhaps help you as you travel down the road to recovery: Keep your mind on things you can control. You will feel like your world is totally out of control. You will drive yourself crazy thinking about them, etc. Don't do that! It will send you "around the bend" quickly. I spent hours thinking about what my (ex) wife and her lover were doing when she wasn't home. It made me physically ill. I finally had to say, "Enough is enough! My physical self will start to reflect my mental state and I cannot let that happen. I need to be strong for my kids!"

Remember that their behavior is not normal. My (ex) wife's behavior was so out of the norm for her, that it was sickening. A high that an affair gives someone is more powerful than the strongest drug that money can buy. It will cause people to do things that they would have never done in a sound mind. My (ex) wife didn't like to drive at night and refused to drive in the snow and ice. One night, she left after dark in a snowstorm to meet her lover. I knew then that there was nothing on this earth to counteract the effects of illicit love.

It is not your fault. While you will be told that it is your fault, remember that it is not. In no way did you drive the other person to do what they did to you. You will hear, "If you would have loved me this way or that way, I would never have left." The important thing to remember is that while you may not have loved them the way they wanted you to, you did love them with all that you had. The offending spouse often forgets that. In addition, they will do anything to justify their abhorrent behavior.

Their life is not better. You will often hear them tell you how great their new life is. It is called justification. You will hear from your kids about how great the new mommy or daddy is because they are being coached or bought off to say how great things are. I remember well the day my girls were so excited that they were getting a new daddy. It broke my heart. But as time has passed, the gem of a new daddy has turned out to be the lump of coal that he is. And my children quickly figured it out.

Take time for yourself. You will need to become aware of your mental as well as physical needs so that you will be there for others. Most often we forget that the two are tied together. Since the divorce rate for second marriages is high (70%), you will need to be there for your kids for their second divorce. Don't be ashamed or feel guilty for saying no to invitations, etc. if it might interfere with the only "me" time that you might have.

And finally, don't let anyone else criticize your ex spouse or call them a name. That is an exclusive right held by you and you only and should be exercised by you only. In my experience, it hurt me to know that my wife left me. But it hurt even more when someone else called them a derogatory name. After all, I chose her to be my wife at one time and I don't want anyone else criticizing my choice. If I made a mistake, I don't need family or friends reminding me." (January 2005)

"More often than not, they think the world is better, greener, easier, more exciting with someone new, then the new person begins to have faults, the sex gets old and less frequent, they gain bills, and the same problems surface. Only unless you fix yourself first and face the things that you need to modify to be in a healthy relationship, will the next relationship be fulfilling. So my point is, it is not about you, it is about THEM! My ex sat in my den crying not 2 months ago, saying he wished he had never done it, he wished he could take it all back, but he knew he had changed everyone's life forever. Most people do regret."(What they have done) (January, 2005).

"My suggestion to everyone and I have to remind myself of this often, is to do something for yourself. Whether it is a spa or a hobby that will take your mind off of your problems for an hour or two a week or daily is great too! Be a volunteer, help someone out even when you don't think you have the strength. The best thing you can do on a day that you find it hard to drag yourself out of bed is to think of something you can do for someone else. That is a great way to remind us, we do have worth! I do in-home day spas where I go in and pamper people and help them to de-stress. At first I thought- I am not the person to do this, but it has turned out to be my way to escape from the crazy life that I have. It gets my mind off of my problems, I meet and interact with people who don't know about my life struggles and it helps me financially so that if I decide I can't continue this madness, I can take care of myself.

It sometimes is not easy to find happiness within ourselves, but it is impossible to find that happiness in someone else. When I feel good about myself, my husband can sense that and it makes him nervous. I think that when they see that we are being torn apart because they hurt us, it makes them feel in control, but when we come across as strong it makes them feel threatened. Read or listen to something encouraging before you go to bed" (January 2005)

"Take it one day at a time. It may take you some time before you cans swim straight and keep your head above water. Once you do though, don't get discouraged when you have "bad" days. They will come when you least expect them." (August 2005)

"I know how you feel and I'm so sorry you have to go through all this. This whole recovery thing is full of setbacks and steps forward. I've been up and down so many times I can't count. Sometimes I get into a funk and just start crying over anything, nothing or everything. It's so hard to stay in control sometimes. Even for us guys who've been taught to "suck it up.' The pain goes beyond anyone's ability to just "get over it" as some self identified experts suggest.

I hate to say, yes, this will continue, but it will. The good news is that it will get better day by day. The downs will be less often and less deep and the ups will last longer and get higher. I understand you feeling embarrassed, (for crying in public) I've done it in "public" as well and it is humiliating. I'm sure they did not think badly of you. They probably were mostly concerned and you do not owe them an explanation. Heck, blame it on PMS or some other sort of thing. Women have far more resources than guys do when it comes to causes of emotional blow outs.
Anyway, my heart goes out to you. I just wish we all did not have to go through all this! (I'm)Thinking of you and wishing you a better day." (August, 2005)

"I focused on my kids. Was I going to show them a pitiful, crying women, or were they going to see someone who could take care of them and myself. I don't feel strong a lot of days, but I keep it from them as much as possible and this helps me in the process. Please hang in there and try to take it one day at a time.
I have had more people (in and out of this group) tell me that life will go on and get better. Hold on to that thought. I don't understand why my husband is doing and saying the things he is, but I am trying to just concentrate on the girls and me right now. I can't control his decisions, but I can do whatever I need to do to make myself feel better." (August, 2005)

"This is probably the toughest challenge you'll ever face in your life. It hurts and it drains you emotionally and physically. The trick is to not let it get the best of you and for you to overcome. Everyone does live through this and is stronger for it. Very little, if any good comes from an affair but in spite of that, we can survive and live a reasonably happy life afterwards. It just takes a lot of time and tears to get there." (August, 2005)

"It's time to stop playing the victim. No one wants to be around someone who is having a pity party all the time. Get a backbone and set some boundaries. You didn't cause this pain to yourself, but you can prolong it. I'm tired of feeling sorry for myself. I want to go days without reliving d-day in my head. I want to trust again. I want to be happy. I feel like sometimes I keep myself down. My husband told me a few days ago that something was different about me. It was self-confidence. That made me smile. He said my new attitude was 'sexy' (first time he has used that word for over a year) I don't walk around crying my eyes out. I have stepped out of my comfort zone, and have started looking forward instead of in the past all the time. Don't get me wrong, I still feel hurt and angry a lot, but it doesn't define me anymore. I'm in a good place (now)." (May, 2005)

"It gets better with time. Just be with your closest friends and DO not just sit at home and feel sorry for yourself. I have been there and done that. When my friends got me out and I started see the world in a single life again, I found that I was better off without my spouse. The hurt and pain will come and go. There will be up and downs, when that happens call your friends at any time. It is what got me over the hurt and pain and now I have having the best time of my life. Everyone needs different time to get over a divorce, but once it's done and over with, you will fill that a weight has been lifted. Life does go on, but in another direction. God will direct you, have faith." (May, 2005)

"Stop worrying about how long it will take the pain to go away and focus on what you're going to do with it. I've heard our pastor speak of "renting space in your head", well; this is where it's a fitting phrase. Life's circumstances can bring us all kinds of happiness and heartaches that linger in our memories. They can serve as motivators to go a certain direction as well as distractions to keep us bogged down at a certain point and unable to focus on anything else. Each of those memories is a tenant we've allowed to take up residence in our heads. But often we forget that it's our head and we are the landlord! Too often we are content to just take the payment of anguish that the hurtful memories want to pay.

Some memories need to stay. They give us useful payments of insight, cherished nuggets of wisdom or happy reflections. Others just need to be evicted! They are going to stay as long as we let them and it's up to us to kick them out. Otherwise, we will continue to have this place in our head that we don't want to go to because of the stench and darkness. We shortchange ourselves and walk around in a funk all day because we don't have full use of what belongs to us. Kick them out!" (April, 2005)

"Choose to make someone else smile & it somehow lifts you up. Cherish what you have, strive for what you want but be grateful for what you do accomplish even if it's short of your original goal. Get up & try again. It is difficult at first but if you sincerely want things to get better, you have to help (yourself). Things won't happen overnight but they will happen. Choose to live, laugh & love. It does work, even if you don't see it right now. Keep on keeping on & the momentum will get you moving until its second nature." (November, 2005)

"I've been thinking a lot about babies lately. I don't know why really. I just have. Maybe it's because they are so innocent and incapable of hurting us. Maybe it's because they don't know how to deceive us.

I do know one thing for sure though. They sure are fun to hug. They are so soft and cuddly and they laugh and giggle a lot. Have you blown on a baby's tummy lately? It's a truly delightful experience. I'm blessed with several babies to choose from (children & grandchildren) with more on the way. When I'm feeling down and out and a little lonely, I try to find a baby to hug and for a few precious moments I forget about the heartache that I have felt for so many years.

Maybe psychologists and counselors should prescribe a new form of therapy: baby hugging. So find a baby somewhere soon and give it a first class hug (I hope) it makes you feel as good as it does me." (December, 2005)

"(Sometimes we wish) death upon ourselves as a better option than the suffering that we have experienced. All of us at one time or other have had similar feelings but, as evidenced by the fact that we are still living, have not acted on these destructive impulses. I pray that you won't either for I truly believe that you and all the other members of our "club" have a lot more to gain by "giving back" than by "giving up." One thing that has helped me, particularly during the Christmas season, is the movie, "It's A Wonderful Life."

The movie stars Jimmy Stewart as George Bailey, the executive who heads up Bailey Bros. Building and Loan. Bailey is unjustly accused of embezzling several thousand dollars which threatens to throw the company into insolvency and Bailey into prison. Bailey is so distraught about the shame that he has brought on his family that he decides suicide is the only answer but is saved from doing so by his guardian angel, Clarence.

Clarence goes to great lengths to show George what a positive effect he has had on the lives of other people and what harm would have come to them if George had never lived. I'm reminded every time I see this movie of how meaningful life can be and how blessed we are to be living it, even during times of hurt and distress." (December, 2005)

"I don't think it's (that you were) a virgin per se that made it so horribly devastating but the fact that you placed her above everyone else and chose to give her your greatest gift you had at the time. It was your most precious offering and the one you loved & trusted with it did not place the same level of importance (if any at all) on it that you did. It's like your favorite toy at Christmas that the next door neighbor just callously breaks & doesn't look back. I believe if you had not been a virgin but she had been your 1st true love, the feelings throughout would have been similar. It's the fact that what we have placed above all else as most important has been trampled by the one we gave it to. I don't think it matters what "IT" is but when it's pulverized by someone we love, it's world tilting & total agony. Every emotional inch of ourselves is changed forever; FOREVER. You can never go back to what was. For some that makes us better, stronger & more prepared for future emotional issues." (January, 2006)

"I am always seeking answers and always come up empty. I feel so helpless when someone like you needs an answer and I can't find it for you or myself. I wish I knew how to tell you to deal with it till the divorce is over but I can't. This much I do know. For the last almost two years, I have thought so many times that I could not go on. I felt that I could not make it another day or bear one more insult to my heart. Yet I somehow seemed to make it. Not without a lot of tears and heartache, but I made it." (January, 2006)

"I don't know how long you have been going through this, but it will only take time (to heal). Some time in the near future you will look up and think, gee-I haven't thought about that crap the whole day, and then it will be a week (you won't have thought about it). Rejection is hard. The loss is worse than a death. Death is natural, with this; the jerk is still out there walking around acting like he has done no wrong. What is maddening is that if you are like me, you actually still miss him and actually think about calling him to laugh about something you just saw on TV or heard from a friend that you are sure would make him laugh. Just know, this grieving is just part of it, (and it too will pass)." (January, 2006)

"My mom has explained to me that in a devastating situation of any type where we can't readily resolve what has caused us such unbearable anguish, our emotional systems whip up anger to provide a barrier of sorts to protect our psyche until such time as we can handle the enormous amount of pain that is laying beneath the anger. It's like the amnesia that some folks experience when something horrible has happened to them when they were young. The mind blocks it out to protect their sanity until they are older & better able to cope with the emotional/mental repercussions. Not much comfort to hear why you feel so bad and not offer a solution I know but at least you know that you are not a bad person, you are perfectly normal. I agree with (the others) & Mom echoes what a lot of us have already found out; it's going to take time." (January, 2006)

"I am enjoying the relationship with my son better than I have in years, am enjoying the process of getting my life in order again and am even beginning a friendship with a man that is very together, emotionally enlightened & tremendously sincere. Things are shining brighter in my life every day I wake up. This can happen for anyone but you must decide it's what you want & not waiver from that course, even when you stumble & take a step back. You get up, stand up straight, look whatever is in front of you in the eye and press forward. You keep doing that until one day you realize you are where you wanted to be and are proud as heck of each & every battle scar because it was YOU who did it all." (March, 2006)

"Guilt is such a useless emotion, and I made some bad decisions because of it. I also think a lot of people in our society assume that the biggest reason for infidelity is that he or she wasn't getting what he or she needed at home and that just makes the guilt worse, especially early on when you don't know how to deal with a lot of what is happening around you. I know there were two people (so called friends) who made me feel that way. Guilt still sneaks in once in awhile, but that is when the serenity prayer comes in very handy." (January, 2006)

"Never, never, never ever feel guilty about an adulterer or adulteress having to suffer the consequences of the affair. They caused the problem and now they can "pay the piper." We are not guilty. They are." (January, 2006)

"It's easy to blame yourself and it never helps when we have a spouse who betrays us and then tells us 100 ways that it was all our fault that he/she did it. We have sort of a mantra that we say over and over; "it's not your fault." They play lots of mind games and then we feel really bad about ourselves. My self esteem hit bottom over my wife's affair, I felt so inadequate and ugly. I agonized and yes, obsessed, day after day over what she had done, seeing her in my mind doing what she did with him. It nearly destroyed me and brought me to the edge of insanity and suicide. If it had not been for my dear friends in our (Beyond Affairs) group I probably would be in much worse shape. You'll find that time does really help heal but it's a long and difficult road. There is hope and you will be ok, that's a promise." (March, 2006)

"I know it's difficult, but try not to be so hard on your self. We may sound strong, but all of us have had our share of bad days. Eventually your good days will out-number your bad ones. I still don't know what sets me in a tail-spin. I will be fine for several weeks and then out of the blue I see or hear something that pulls all of the baggage back into the open again. How do I feel about this new chapter in my life? I Feel excited, scared, worried, tired, at peace; all of the above. You can and will get through this. Guard your heart and take care." (March, 2006)

"I don't know if the sense of loss will ever end completely. (But) it is getting easier for me. My old family, that included my husband, was full of traditions. My counselor has suggested that I try to create as many new traditions as possible to help mentally replace the old ones. Christmas was difficult, but we packed in as many activities as we could handle. Being a new family of three females, our family outings are now much more "girlie." It is a lot of work to plan these outings, but as my older daughter said recently, "Sometimes, it feels like it has always just been the three of us." I want their father to stay a part of their lives, but that doesn't mean we have to stay locked in our old roles. He is the one that will eventually experience a loss even greater than mine. We three girls have had to lean on each other, and therefore the bond between us has become extremely tight. That is something my husband will never be able to take away from us."(March, 2006)

"You are not alone in how you feel but it will get better. We have all been upset, lonely and scared. We have also been bitter, vengeful, resentful, etc. We have also wept and cried until we could not cry anymore. These are all natural reactions to what you have experienced. In fact, I feel that we would not be human if we reacted with complete and total indifference. As time goes on the pain will begin to dissipate. In order to speed up the healing, please stay in contact (with those who can support you), get good counseling, communicate, don't push your feelings down, and above all don't withdraw and isolate yourself." (March, 2006)

"It isn't easy and it often seems that there are road blocks no matter which way you go. All I can suggest is that you follow your heart, as no matter what you chose to do, there will be people that will criticize or judge or think they would have done things better than you (and these are the people that love us!!) When I fight, I am told I should have taken the more conservative road....if I take the conservative road, I am told I should have fought.....even when I follow their advice, they will turn around and say I should have done it differently! You just can't win, so you have to be true to yourself. Don't try to please others, please yourself." (March, 2006)

"Don't worry about the money, the house or anything that you have or own. And don't ever focus on what others are telling you who have not ever been in a situation similar to yours. You need to focus on your mental and physical health. If you will feel better mentally or physically by staying, then do so. If leaving will make you feel better, then leave. Before my divorce, I worried about the house, money and debt. My wife's affair and our divorce brought in to focus how fleeting and unimportant possessions can be. I lost a lot of stuff in my divorce and honestly, I don't miss it. And I no longer hoard money like a squirrel collecting nuts while preparing for a long hard winter. Am I foolish with money? I don't think so. I have just come to understand that certain things have to happen before goals can be met. You might see that you will need to sacrifice, scrimp and save and maybe go into some debt in order to plant the seeds for bigger, better goals. But if I can say anything, it is that your mental and physical health is of paramount importance. Sure money buys "stuff" but it can't buy peace of mind." (March, 2006)

"What it (a divorce) has done for me personally is that I will always be able to look back and know that I did the right thing, I made every effort to fix the marriage, I did everything possible, so the failure of the marriage, in my opinion is ALL on him.. I will never have to look at my step son and say - I am sorry, maybe if I would have stayed longer, maybe if I could have done this or that. I can look him in the face, when he is older, and say - "I did everything I could to save our family, but when it became more devastating to stay the course, I had to make changes so I could be the person God made me to be; for me and for the people he put in my life". (May, 2006)

"I don't have to carry that load of guilt. If my marriage doesn't survive, I can move forward to other relationships and hold my head high. Whatever "price" I might pay for keeping the high road is not nearly the price my husband has paid for taking the low road - whether he sees that or not. The choice that those of us whose spouse didn't leave have to make afterwards is whether the relationship is worth salvaging or whether we need to move on. Like you said, sometimes there are more questions than answers. In the end, each of us has to decide whether to keep working on the relationship or when it is time to move on in life. Keep searching and the answers will come to you. God bless!" (May, 2006)

"The good news is that I feel like I have moved past 95% of the hurt, pain, and dismay of the affair. I have started dating again, and have been made to feel desirable and have worth. I had to acquire these feelings for myself first before I could accept them from other people. The long separation (before the divorce) (15 months) with no dating forced me to make my own happiness. Dating feels a little strange after being with the same person for 18 years, but it's been fun. It does get better!" (June, 2006)

All of us who have been through what you are experiencing hope that you will find your way to a happier and better life. Thinking of the past will only delay your healing. It is done, over with, kaput! The future is where your happiness lies so get with it and plan that better life now. It is waiting for you; all you need do is start the journey and you'll soon be there. God bless you and good luck in your recovery. (August, 2006)

The Best Books

Reading is one of the most therapeutic activities that you can engage in at this stage of your recovery. There are so many good (and many bad) books on the subject of affairs by scholars, clergy, researchers and professionals that the bookshelf can be quite intimidating. Reading some of the best books on the subject will allow you to step outside of your life and look at the issue in a more clinical, less personal way. Seeing what others have to say about why affairs happen and understanding the process of rebuilding can work wonders in helping you sort out things. It also offers a great deal of comfort to see (beyond what I've said) that you are not alone in your feelings, challenges and the pain you are feeling. Somehow, just knowing you are "normal" is of great relief. I've read many books on the subject and so too have the people in my support group. This list is intentionally limited so as to not overwhelm and to provide the very best information. If you want to go beyond this list, by all means do so. From our combined reading, I offer you these books as "the best of the best" and ones I feel are of the most help.

The Monogamy Myth,

A Personal Handbook for Recovering from Affairs, 3rd Edition
Vaughan, Peggy
2003, Newmarket Press, NY.
ISBN 1-55704-542-9

Review of The Monogamy Myth, by the author:
"I take great pride in this book because the ideas it contains come NOT from my personal opinions about affairs—but from having faithfully organized and reported the information received from the hundreds of people who shared their stories with me after I went public with my own story back in 1980. This allowed me to identify the general patterns involved in dealing with affairs and to get greater understanding of what works and what doesn't. This book was originally published in 1989, with an updated edition in 1998 and another update in January, 2003. However, these updates required only adding material about online affairs, about our BAN Support Group and providing additional resources for help in recovering. There were NO changes required in the original material. The solid nature of the information in the book has stood the test of time. Finally, I want to take this opportunity to draw attention to the fact that while this book is a vital resource for those personally facing this issue, it is an excellent source of information and perspective for friends and family AND for the general public who could benefit from understanding more about this difficult issue that affects so many people."

That said, for many of us this book is the holy grail of knowledge and understanding of affairs. Vaughan has established herself as the most well known expert on the subject and her careful and thorough research is the most extensive done on the subject to date. I and almost all of the members of our group have found this book to be the most helpful in understanding affairs and in its insights into our own struggles. It is a must read! If you can only read one book on affairs, this must be the one. This book also had the most positive effect on my wife and it presents a very fair and balanced look at both sides of the affair equation.

Torn Asunder

Recovering From Extramarital Affairs (Revised Edition)
Carder, Dave & Jaenicke, Duncan
1995, Moody Press (Christian)
ISBN 0-8024-7748-8

This was the very first book I read after D-day. It offered me a great deal of insight into the reasons people have affairs, the kinds of affairs and the recovery process. I found it very helpful. The author uses a number of examples and "exercises" that can help a couple rebuild. He also offers good advice as to deciding whether to stay or leave the marriage and how to deal with children. Mr. Carder's counseling approach and process for recovery is perhaps the most successful and insightful in practice today. Carder is a pastor and the book is Christian in its approach. I rank this one in my top three.

After the Affair:

Healing the Pain and Rebuilding Trust When a Partner Has Been Unfaithful
Spring, Janis A.
1996, Harper Publishers, NY
ISBN 0-06-92817-4

I've read this one and personally found it helpful, so too did my wife. It gets mixed reviews from readers at Amazon.com, some loved it and some did not. Publishers Weekly said: "For married or cohabiting couples who want to rebuild their relationship after one partner had had an affair, this tough-minded, insightful manual will be eminently practical. Clinical psychologist Spring, writing with her husband, draws on 20 years of experience treating distressed couples as she explains how both the unfaithful partner and the betrayed one can confront their doubts and fears about recommitting, constructively communicate pain and anger, restore trust, renew sexual intimacy and forgive."

As for my opinion, this book is second only to Peggy Vaughan's *The Monogamy Myth* in providing a very balanced look at both sides of the issues and will help you understand some of the issues (not your fault) that lead people into affairs. Dr. Spring's approach is a little more clinical than Vaughan's book but still is a very worthwhile read.

Solo Partner, The

Repairing your relationship on your own.
Deluca, Phil
1996, Hartley & Marks Publishers, Vancouver, BC
ISBN 0-88179-129-6

This book was recommended to me by my counselor during the period when my wife was being very unhelpful and resisting my efforts to heal things. The book is out of print and copies are hard to come by but it is worth finding. EBay is your most likely source. The book is for anyone who is trying to repair a relationship and their partner is uncooperative. The premise is that even without cooperation, you can take personal responsibility for fixing things. It gave me tremendous insight into my anger and how many of my own actions were preventing reconciliation. It also gave me insights into how "her" actions were blocking reconciliation. The book provides powerful techniques that work. It also must be kept entirely to yourself. If your partner knows your plan, they can surely defeat it. It was startling to me how quickly some of the recommended techniques got me results.

My Husband's Affair Became the Best Thing That Happened to Me
Bercht, Anne with Brian and Danielle Bercht
2004, Trafford Publishing, Victoria, BC
ISBN: 1412033209

This book is one of the best and most inspiring "first person" accounts of an affair, its consequences and the couple's road to recovery. The author is the current International coordinator of the Beyond Affairs Network. A unique aspect of this book is the accounts by not only the author but her husband, Brian who had the affair and their daughter Danielle. With their contributions, the impacts of an affair on an entire family can be clearly seen. The following reader comments are from the publisher's web page for the book. (trafford.com/robots/04-1147.html)

This book makes a wonderful contribution to the growing willingness of couples to "break the code of silence" and share their experience with affairs in order to help others. It offers clear insight into the pain involved as well as great hope for the power to recover and rebuild the marriage.
Peggy Vaughan, author of "The Monogamy Myth," and Host of dearpeggy.com

What a ride! Anne captures her marital journey in a way that leaves you feeling as if you've just completed a double loop on a roller coaster...only to realize there's another one coming! After reading their story, I see Anne and Brian as champions of honesty,

commitment, perseverance....and true love.
Monica Columbus - A Reader

Love Must Be Tough & Straight Talk

(Available as a Double book or singly)
Dobson, James C.
1996, Word Publishing, Nashville, TN
ISBN 0-8499-1654-2

Book synopsis from Amazon.com: "This two-in-one volume contains the classic James Dobson bestsellers *Love Must Be Tough* and *Straight Talk*—each loaded with practical, straightforward advice for relationship building. In *Love Must Be Tough*, Dr. Dobson attacks the root problem of most marital crises—a lack of respect—offering practical help for rekindling mutual respect and mature love. *Straight Talk* stakes a clear path through the confusion of men's roles, teaching men how to build stable, loving and satisfying relationships with their wives and children. Thousands of lives have been dramatically changed though the principles presented in these essential books which are now together for the first time ever." Of the two in this double book, *Love Must Be Tough* is the best. Every review of this book describes it in glowing terms. Everyone in my support group who has read the book loves it and it is one of the most recommended books in our library.

Private Lies

Pittman, Frank
1989, W. W. Norton Co., NYC
ISBN 0-393-30707-7

I found this book very interesting, partly because my wife's infidelity was also laced with a compulsive habit of lying about almost everything and also because the book provides insights into deception and types of affairs that many other books miss. If you want to expand your view of infidelity and explore the role that lies play in relationships, I highly recommend this book. The book outlines the patterns of betrayal that Pittman encountered in his practice and helps us understand and debunk many of the popular myths about affairs.

The book has mixed reviews from readers on Amazon.com and interestingly, most of the negatives are from those who've had affairs. That in itself should be the best recommendation of all. The truth hurts.

Not Just Friends

Rebuilding Trust and Recovering Your Sanity after Infidelity
Glass, Shirley P., PhD
2003, Free Press, N. Y.
ISBN 0-7432-2550-3 (Softback)

If you've wondered about a relationship your partner has with someone of the opposite sex and they've told you they are "just friends." You must read this book right away. Though this book's title states it is an "after infidelity" issue, for most of us who have read it, it seems more a "preventive" book. However, that said, Glass does address many of the recovery issues and helps explain why affairs happen. Glass explains how work related friendships often result in affairs. She also offers terrific advice on how to avoid an affair. While one such author states that one should completely avoid friendships with the opposite sex, Glass gives advice on how to control relationships and how to stay out of an unwanted entanglement. Since a huge percentage of affairs happen at work, this is a must read for anyone who has not yet fallen into an affair. For those who already have, the book offers understanding of why and helps your recovery. This is a highly acclaimed book and all of the people in my support group have praised it.

Of course there are many more books of merit on the subject of affairs and if you are a voracious reader, by all means, read all that you can. This list represents my short list of the best books on the subject and ones that I believe will help you understand what might have happened in your own relationship and guide you towards your long term recovery. Once you are on the road to recovery it is critical that if you are reconciling your relationship, preventing future affairs be a major objective. At that point, the following book is a must have!

Preventing Affairs

You CAN have a monogamous marriage but not just by assuming you are immune.
Vaughan, Peggy
2008, Dialog Press, San Diego

At this writing *Preventing Affairs* is available as an E-book in PDF format at preventingaffairs.com and is available in print at Amazon.com as of July, 2008.

The Best Internet Sites

I mentioned before that the Internet is both a blessing and a curse. That is true in almost any area of information and affairs are no exception. Any of us (including me) can establish a website and publish anything we want. In many cases, what you read on the net is opinion or pure fabrication and you should always be cautious about the sources of the material you find.

When I first discovered my wife's infidelity, I immediately began searching for help on the net. Later, after having read quality books by certified experts and getting involved in the Beyond Affairs Network, I continued searching for information and found that there are many sites out there that are exceptionally good and many that are exceptionally bad.

The problem is that some of the bad ones were written by otherwise intelligent people who simply did not have a clue. In general, the best sites are those that are either written by or include contributions from people who have really been there. Psychologists, counselors and other "experts" who have not actually experienced what we have can only relate through what they read and what they hear from their patients. Though their education and intelligence prepares them to effectively try to understand, there is nothing like "being there." What they can do is listen and help you deal with the emotional damage.

Some health care professionals may disagree but I liken it to war. You can read about war, you can watch movies or TV documentaries and you can listen to first hand accounts and think you now understand what war is like. But, till you are there, in the jungle or desert with a rifle in your hand and bullets screaming past your head, you'll never understand the depth of feelings and the emotional truths one faces in war. The same is true of affairs. Only those who have been there can understand the depth of emotional pain and what really works to deal with it.

The following websites have been recommended by people in my support group and me as quality sources of information about affairs and recovery. They contain few errors in understanding and provide information and comfort. I add one caution, the sites that are "chat" sites or include chat functions must be approached with an understanding that the chat information is coming from the general population and as such, there can be some exceptionally bad advice. Even though these people have been there, some of them still manage to pass on bad advice.

Also, be aware that the web is populated by thousands of predators and "trolls." These people like nothing better than making up false identities and playing mind games with vulnerable people. Never make direct contact with someone on a chat site and do not use your real name or email address. Some of these individuals haunt these sites looking for vulnerable people that they can prey on in the hopes of making physical contact. Some come just to say nasty things and annoy others. Be cautious and as you visit them, you will see what I mean.

DearPeggy.com (Founding Home of the Beyond Affairs Network) – dearpeggy.com

This is the mother of all affair help sites and provides you with plenty of specific articles that will help you understand affairs and recovery. Peggy's "Question of the Week" feature is interesting and informative. You can purchase PDF copies her books and compilations of the questions of the week for nominal prices. Quite honestly, this site is the best and most informative you will find and I would say it will provide you with all you need to know except for "chat" with others.

Beyond Affairs – (Current Home of Beyond Affairs Network) beyondaffairs.com/

This is the site that in June of 2006 became the sponsoring site for the Beyond Affairs Network. This site hosts the BAN network now that Peggy Vaughan has retired from active management of the network. It also contains a great deal of helpful information about dealing with affairs and the site owners, Anne & Brian Bercht, offer excellent books and seminars.

Surviving Infidelity - survivinginfidelity.com/

This is the best affair related chat site on the net. It also includes some reading resources and help information. The chat forums are monitored and they have a solid set of "rules" that are enforced vigorously. Some of the reading material submitted by some members is a little off base but overall, this site nets a high recommendation. The many useful and targeted forums include one for those who committed adultery and will give you some first hand insights into those who betray us. This is probably the only infidelity chat site you will ever need. You'll have to register but can choose a "screen name" that protects your identity. In all cases when registering at chat sites, be sure to select the option that masks your email address.

2-in-2-1 Marriage Clinic - 2-in-2-1.co.uk/marriageclinic/infidelity/

A great site full of resource links. Check out the signs of infidelity-even if the affair is over & you are rebuilding; it is good to know the signs (many I didn't pick up on) in order to catch the clues before there is a repeat of the pain & emotional devastation.

AdultHoodWonderful.com

adulthoodwonderful.com/survive%20affairs/infidelity.htm

Adulthoodwonderful.com has a section on infidelity; it offers information on signs of infidelity, how people cheat and other help subjects.

ChatCheaters.com - chatcheaters.com

Since cyber affairs are just as destructive as real life ones; this link may help those affected with the question of "how do I compete with a fantasy?" I found the information on self esteem relevant to all survivors of affairs whether real life or cyber.

ConsciousLoving.com - consciousloving.com

One of my support group members says about this site: "This was the very first site I found when I discovered the betrayal. I still visit it daily. The articles are superb and once you are ready the forums and message boards are a good way of getting multiple perspectives on every relationship issue. This is not just an infidelity site but a site for those looking to consciously learn to live & love. Marriage, Dating, Sexual matters and concerns, Relationship successes, Relationship challenges, etc are all available on multiple sub-forums. This is a big site with so much information that you will find helpful."

How To Prevent Affairs -

beyondaffairs.com/articles/preventing_affairs.htm.

This is a short but pithy article written by Anne Bercht, owner and author of the above mentioned "Beyond Affairs" website. This article is quoted from her book "My Husband's Affair was the Best Thing That Happened to Me." The article gets down to the basics of what a couple should do to prevent affairs. Perhaps not useful for what has happened to us, but should be something we all should consider in all of our future relationships.

Ivillage.com - ivillage.com/

Ivillage.com has a number of articles about affairs and relationships. Though this site says it is for women, I think men can gain much insight by reading the articles.

How To Select A Counselor -
johnfishbein.com/FeelBetterFast/Fishbein/how.to.select.html

This site guides you in how to select a counselor with good advice from a professional. Peggy Vaughan's site, dearpeggy.com has very affair specific help on this subject.

Marriage Builders - marriagebuilders.com/

This is an excellent site for those who are going to try to repair a marriage in trouble or those who want to solidify an already healthy marriage.

Network54 Affair Chat Forum -
network54.com/Forum/90639/

Recovering from Affairs, this is a chat forum about affair recovery and general questions.

SexInfo101.com - sexinfo101.com/index.shtml

If you are interested in revitalizing your sex life; CAUTION, definitely contains explicit material! Ivillage & Marriage Builders have a lot of good advice in this area too.

Straight Spouse Network - ssnetwk.org/

For those whose spouse has had a homosexual affair. The Straight Spouse Network is a worldwide organization of current/

former heterosexual spouses/partners of gay, lesbian, bisexual, or transgender mates and mixed-orientation couples. Members provide personal, confidential support and resource information to spouses, couples, and families. SSN is the only support network of its kind in the world.

Understanding Sexual Addiction -
understandingsexualaddiction.org

For those who are either married to or suffering from sexual or love addiction; this site has a lot of enlightening information, quizzes and keys for staying faithful while overcoming the addiction. There are separate free e-courses for the addict, the partner and the couple.

Seeking Professional Help

This may be the last chapter of this book but by no means is it the least important; in fact, seeking professional help in the form of counseling or psychiatric support may well be the most important aspect of your recovery. I know you've seen many suggestions throughout the book to seek professional help for many situations. Counseling is a nearly universal need for those of us who have been betrayed by infidelity due to the terrible emotional consequences we suffer. Selecting someone to help you should not be a random act. You should be somewhat discriminating and selective before committing to a long term process with a counselor.

The important reason for being careful is that quite honestly, when it comes to handling the issue of infidelity, not all counselors are equally proficient. Certainly all are well educated and in most states are licensed. They are well versed in counseling processes and handling emotional and most marital problems but it seems many of them carry many misperceptions about infidelity and many also fail to recognize the extreme depth of devastation that comes with it.

Many of the people I've associated with who have been to counseling have been dissatisfied with the help (or lack thereof) that they received. Many found that a counselor was all too willing to first blame the betrayed one for some marital failure. Doing so has horrible consequences. Some don't seem to get the "it's not your fault" concept and dive right into having you look at what terrible things you did to drive your partner into someone else's arms. Many therapists often assume that the cause of the infidelity is because we failed to meet some unspoken need and what else could you expect but for your partner to meet those needs elsewhere. I could go on and on but the main point is that some counselors are simply clueless when it comes to how to deal with infidelity or what causes it.

I do not want to imply that this failure is found in the majority of counselors but research and anecdotal evidence implies it is more widespread than we would like to think.

In 2002, Peggy Vaughan conducted a groundbreaking and significant survey that examined among other things, the state of counseling as it relates to the issue of infidelity. This survey and guidance for therapists and their clients (us) was published in a very useful e-book, *Help for Therapists (And Their Clients) in Dealing with Affairs*. The book is available in PDF format at dearpeggy.com in the bookstore. The survey was of over 1,000 people who have been betrayed by an affair and their experiences in dealing with the aftermath of an affair. Of the respondents, 75% were women and 25% men. That survey brought a number of important issues to light that all of us seeking help should be aware of.

In essence, the survey found that some counselors tend to want to deal with affairs as a general marital problem rather than dealing directly with affairs. Some tend to overlook the emotional devastation and jump to solutions. This is what my first counselor did to me and I was not ready for rational thought, I needed immediate help with the emotional consequences. The respondents noted that many counselors tried to place blame, usually on the offended spouse. The respondents went on to make more suggestions that included:

- Don't believe everything the one who had the affair tells you.
- Help "us" connect with others who have had the same experience (The purpose of the BAN groups)

- Be more informed about affairs
- Encourage honesty
- Be supportive of those who want to "save" the marriage. (Unfortunately, many therapists focus on separation and ultimate dissolution of the relationship)
- Do not allow your (the therapist's) own gender biases to interfere with your judgment of either party or what happened.

My first counselor put all his focus on readying me to be able to leave my wife. When I refused to do so he rather rudely told me there was nothing more he could do for me and that was the last I saw of him. He never dealt with my emotional needs and I ended my time with him no better off than I started other than being prepared to leave my wife which I did not want to do. All of this is an indication that many therapists are not prepared to effectively deal with the aftermath of affairs so it is important that you be selective in your search for a therapist.

Once again, Peggy Vaughn provides us with some guidance on this issue through some of her articles and excerpts from speech by a therapist (William J. Doherty, Ph.D) regarding questions to ask a potential therapist. His suggestion to "screen" a potential therapist is excellent advice. From what I have personally seen and heard from others, it is absolutely critical that you find a therapist who understands affairs and who has some experience in counseling couples or individuals. His suggestion is to call ahead or on your first meeting to ask some targeted questions. Among his suggestions for screening are:

"Can you describe your background and training in marital therapy?"

If the therapist is self-taught or workshop-trained, and can't point to a significant education in this work, then consider going elsewhere.

"What is your attitude toward salvaging a trouble marriage versus helping couples break up?"

If the therapist says he or she is "neutral," or "I don't try to save marriage, I try to help people" look elsewhere. (I'd also run if the therapist says he or she does not believe in divorce.)

"What is your approach when one partner is seriously considering ending the marriage and the other wants to save it?"

If the therapist responds by focusing only on helping each person clarify their personal feelings and decisions, consider looking elsewhere.

"What percentage of your practice is marital therapy?"

Avoid therapists who mostly do individual therapy.

"Of the couples you treat, what percentage would you say work out enough of their problems to stay married with a reasonable amount of satisfaction with the relationship."
--"What percentage break up while they are seeing you?"
--"What percentage do not improve?"
--"What do you think makes the differences in these results?"

If someone says "100%" stay together, I would be

concerned, and if they say that staying together is not a measure of success for them, I'd be concerned."

If you would like to read Dr. Doherty's entire speech, you can find it at: smartmarriages.com/hazardous.html. The title of the speech is: *How Therapy Can Be Hazardous To Your Marital Health.*

In addition to his suggestions, I would add that you should also ask if the counselor has actually personally been affected by an affair or even if he/she has had one. They may not tell but if they do it can offer some additional guidance. Obviously, if they have been betrayed, they will understand much more than someone who has not. If they were one who had an affair, I'd further explore their beliefs. Personally, I'd be uncomfortable with one who had an affair, they could be much more supportive of the rationalizations of your partner. I would then ask some questions related to the failings I've outlined above. Here are some possible other questions more related to affairs and the therapist's experience or beliefs.

- Do you believe an affair is a failure of one person to give their partner what they need?
- Do you think that those who have had an affair are sometimes justified in doing so?
- What experience have you had in counseling individuals and couples in recovering from an affair?
- Do you believe that an affair is a result of marital problems or are there other causes.
- How do you first approach counseling with someone (or a couple) that have experienced infidelity?

You should choose some, not necessarily all of these suggested questions so as to not turn the call or first meeting into an interrogation but you should tell the therapist that you want to be sure that there is a good fit for you and (if involved) your spouse. Most should understand that and you certainly owe it to yourself to be sure you have someone who is most likely to help you and deal with the important issues rather than blame you.

The dearpeggy.com site has started a list of recommended therapists in areas around the country. These are people who have experience in affairs and who have positively helped others like you and I. The list currently has over 200 qualified and recommended therapists in the US and some for other countries. Though the list is still limited, we hope that over time there may be many more. The list is at:

dearpeggy.com/therapists.html

As mentioned elsewhere in my book, you sometimes need more than just a counselor and you should seek the appropriate level of help depending on your situation. If your emotional trauma and psychological state is extreme, consider a psychologist or psychiatrist. If you are dealing with serious thoughts about suicide, do the same and in addition, connect with a suicide help line or support group in your area. You can find a listing of such groups on the internet at: suicide.org/suicide-support-groups.html.

Appendix

Some Possible Answers to Questions in the "Dealing with" Chapters.

As you worked your way through this book, several of the chapters included self examination questions to allow you to explore your own feelings and thoughts about the issue at hand. In most cases, the answers are reflective of your own feelings and the only "right" answer is your own. In other cases, there are some answers that may generalize the issue but again, are not necessarily the "right" answer. The answers provided here are only suggestions as to possible answers and are given here simply for general guidance, to help you get started in those cases where you may be temporarily drawing a blank or just to give you a different perspective. In many cases, the text following the questions in the chapters where they appear actually provides alternative answers.

Chapter 6: Dealing with Your Anger.

What good do you think comes out of anger?

Very little good comes out of anger that lasts longer than a short time. In the short term, sometimes anger helps release tension and allows you to "let off steam." That can be helpful. Sometimes anger can help you deal with an immediate frustration or to purge some intense feelings but on balance, very little if any real good comes out of anger.

What negative consequences are there?

Though little good comes from anger, the negative consequences are many. The text of the chapter lays them out pretty well but it may help to restate them. Anger can lead to serious physical and mental health problems, mostly related to the stress induced by anger. It also can lead to serious bodily injury or even incarceration if you carry the anger to the point of overt action against someone or even yourself.

Do you know the signs of when your alligator is taking over? (What physical and mental feelings do you have when you begin to get angry?)

The answer to this question is a personal one but if you've never thought it over before and are having a hard time sorting out the feelings, these possibilities may help you in determining your own signals of impending loss of control through anger. A tightening of muscles or in the stomach area can be an indicator, sweating, clenching of fists, tightening of the jaw, bulging eyes and a hard stare can all be signals. A rise of pitch and loudness of your voice can often presage loss of control. Confusion or unsteadiness, actually seeing stars, inability to think clearly can all be mental indicators. Search your own past and see if you can identify times when you became angry and out of control and try to remember what you felt or thought. Identify those feelings and be tuned in to your own reactions to recognize an onset of anger and stop it from going out of control.

What productive ways have worked for you in the past to process or reduce your anger?

Productive ways to process anger involve using the energy generated in constructive rather than destructive ways. In many cases brisk exercise or heavy physical exertion can quickly burn off the negative energy and adrenaline burst that accompanies anger. As suggested in the chapter, even taking a bat to a photo of the one you are angry with or a punching bag can be very cathartic. Once you've taken care of diverting the negative energy, you should try to examine what lead to the outburst and look for ways to control it or divert it before it gets out of control.

What advice would you offer to others who are dealing with anger?

This of course is one of those "your answer is best" questions. Take what you learn about yourself or from this chapter and help others whom you know might have anger problems. Sometimes helping others can also be an effective way to heal yourself and control your own anger by setting examples for others.

Chapter 7: Dealing with Depression.

Do you think you suffer from a form of clinical depression?

This question is one only you can answer. The ultimate authority would be a health care professional. The purpose of it is a sort of "head check" to get you thinking about your own mental state. If you are experiencing some of the symptoms outlined in the chapter that indicate clinical depression, you must see a professional.

What symptoms are you personally experiencing?

This question also is a personal one, a chance for you to think about your current state of mind and health and to take an inventory of your symptoms (if any) related to possible depression. Don't skip over this question; it is important that you stay in tune with your own health.

At what point would you consider seeing a psychiatrist, counselor or physician to help you with your depression?

Aside from testing your own tolerance and self examining your willingness to seek help, you should absolutely seek professional help if you have thoughts of suicide, dangerous malicious tendencies towards others, find yourself suffering from sleep deprivation, suffering from too much sleep (usually a sign of escape from reality) are missing work and other obligations due to emotional upset, taking non-prescribed or illegal drugs or feeling chest pains or other heath related signs. Review the list of symptoms in the chapter and if you find you have them, seek help.

How do you feel about using prescribed drugs to treat your depression?

Again, this is a "head check" for you to consciously think about your beliefs regarding the value of prescribed medications to help you with your depression. Some people resist such actions for various reasons. If you find yourself resistant to the idea, ask your health care professional and discuss it with them. Personally, I have been helped significantly by medication and the vast majority of those in my group who have availed themselves of medication also believe they are helpful and that the benefits are well worth it. However, my opinion or that of others can not replace an honest discussion and the advice of a health care professional.

Besides these options, what have you been able to personally do to make you less depressed?

If you come up blank on this question then you should go back and look at the suggestions in this (Depression) chapter. If you've come up with some new ideas that work for you, let me know and I'll add them to the list in the next edition!

Chapter 8: Dealing with Obsessive Thoughts.

Do recurring undesired thoughts related to your partner's affair haunt you?

This is almost universal for all of us who have been betrayed. Answering "yes" to this question in some ways should be reassuring that you are not abnormal in having these thoughts. We all have them and for many of us it is the most difficult obstacle to overcome.

What are some of your most recurring obsessive thoughts?

As with many other questions, only you can answer this. It is your opportunity to take an inventory of your own issues and be consciously aware of them and the power they currently hold over you. Once you know, you can face them head-on.

What are some of the triggers that start your obsessive thoughts?

Though this is another question that only you can answer, it is important to be aware of what triggers your obsessive thoughts. Being aware of them allows you to either be prepared when you know you will be in a situation that may trigger them or avoid situations and subjects that may trigger them.

What have you personally done that seems effective in controlling your obsessive thoughts?

This is another opportunity to consciously think about things that have helped you deal with obsession. By openly noting what works, you may be more apt to remember the technique(s) when you begin having obsessive thoughts. If you have some unique ideas that work, let me know about them by emailing me at firstaid@bellsouth.net.

Chapter 9: Dealing With the Shock and Stress

How did you feel after discovery of your partner's affair and what were some of the "symptoms" or behaviors you experienced?

This question is to help you to clearly identify some of the feelings you have experienced as a result of discovery. Some possible (but not all) common feelings are sadness, anger, fear, panic, disbelief, nausea, physical pain (such as headache or muscle spasms), inability to think clearly, withdrawal, sleeping too much and of course a general state of shock.

What are some options that you think might help a person overcome stress disorders?

There are a number of ideas in the chapter on this subject; hopefully some of them will be personally helpful. More often than not, getting involved in activities that are physical, mentally challenging or focused on helping others can move you away from your own troubles or divert energy into more productive ways. If you have a hobby or special skill (such as music, dancing or painting) that you enjoy, immersing yourself in it regularly adds a level of enjoyment that can relieve stress and give you a mental break from all the stress.

What has worked for you in reducing the effects of stress on your own life?

As with all the other similar questions, this is another opportunity to consciously think about things that have helped you deal with this issue (stress). By openly noting what works, you may be more apt to remember the technique(s) when you begin having obsessive thoughts. If you have some unique ideas that work, let me know about them by emailing me at firstaid@bellsouth.net.

Chapter 10: Restoring Your Self Esteem.

How did you feel after discovery of your partner's affair?

If you are like the rest of us, you felt pretty worthless and down in the dumps to say the least. It is not uncommon to immediately have feelings of worthlessness, undesirability and failure. There are a myriad of feelings so just use this opportunity to purge the thoughts you've had about yourself. In doing so, the hope is that you'll be better able to look at them rationally and eliminate them.

What sort of thoughts did you have about yourself?

This is nothing more than a "drill down" related to the preceding question to focus on your self esteem related reactions. Only you know the answers that relate to yourself.

What are some unhealthy ways to try to rebuild?

I think a main point here is that anything that you do that does not refute the feelings of worthlessness or failure related to this incident is not healthy, nor is it rebuilding. Actions that magnify these negative feelings such as continually feeling sorry for yourself or repeating the negatives you hear from your partner are destructive and rebuild the negatives rather than the positives about yourself. It is unhealthy to believe the worst about your self and the only way to "rebuild" is to refute the feelings and focus on the truth.

What else, besides your partner's opinion and actions defines your self worth?

It is important to look across the entire spectrum of your life and look at more than one person's opinion. This is especially true if the person is someone trying to justify what they did. Your self worth is most often defined by your own thoughts but often that is guided by other people's actions for or against you. Think of the times when other's have supported you, praised you r expressed appreciation. Think of things you do well and special skills or abilities you have and balance them against the negatives you are hearing from your partner. Take personal pride of the things you do well and your personal moral and ethical compass and realize that you are not worthless and this one person or no other person's opinion defines you. In fact, in most cases, the adulterer says many things that are not true about you to make them feel better about what they did. It is a very mean and unfair trade-off. You define yourself.

What examples can you think of where your inner voice worked against your success?

Try to remember times when you talked yourself out of success or into thinking you could not accomplish something. All of us do that at one time or another (except perhaps Donald Trump) and it is not a defect to admit this. The important point here is to see that your inner voice often works against you, sometimes more often that for you. As a comparison, try to think of times when your inner voice helped. Regardless, try not to listen to that negative voice within you and teach it to be more positive.

Is the inner voice always logically correct?

Unless your inner voice expresses sentiments of success and positive outcomes, chances are it is always wrong. Use the inner voice to encourage yourself rather than discourage.

Chapter 11: Rebuilding Trust

Everyone seems to say it takes time to rebuild trust, are there things we do to slow it down? Can we speed it up?

Much of what we do after being betrayed can either rebuild or prevent the re-establishment of trust. It is indeed very difficult to even think about once again trusting the person who betrayed us.

It does take time and so much has to do with how your partner behaves from now on. At that point, you can either prevent a rebuilding or help it. You can hinder trust by constantly reminding the person that they betrayed you. That will set up a roadblock and my even deter them from trying. You should remain open or at least neutral to allowing the person to prove themselves. You can also encourage it by letting them know you appreciate their honesty whenever it is clear they have done so. You'll never take things at face value again but don't be so mistrusting that you "investigate" everything or distrust everything. Pick your issues carefully and let your partner know you are willing to give them a chance to prove they can be trusted again. However, I know you will never rebuild to a situation of blind trust. You tried that once and it failed. Keep your antennas up.

Has your experience given you the ability to better assess the level of trustworthiness of other people? If so, in what ways?

In discussing this issue with many people in our situation, nearly all now realize that blind trust or taking things at face value is not wise. We now have learned the hard lesson that full trust can be hazardous. For most of us, that wariness extends to meeting other people and if single again, getting to know people better before investing too much in the relationship. You now know that many of the "gut" feelings you had about your partner were right. You also know you missed or ignored many important clues as to strange goings on out of trust or love. You also know now that most people present a different side of themselves when they are trying to "hook up" with someone. Use those lessons to be more critical and rational in assessing what others tell you or represent to you as the truth. You do not want to become a cynic who believes no-one but you do want to use your intelligence rather than emotion to judge others from now on.

Are there things that you can do as you develop new relationships to assess the level of trust you can put in others?

This can be difficult. You do not want to seem to mistrust everything someone tells you and you do not want it to appear you are testing them on everything. However, you can take many things with a grain of salt and spend more time getting to know the person. If there are details that seem suspicious, go ahead and either ask questions or if you think it is necessary, seek confirmation through other methods. Ask to meet some of his/her friends and get to know them well. They may be able to provide insights. Sometimes just mentioning something the person of interest told you to them can get a telling reaction. Just take it slow and easy and be sure the person is being honest with you. If not, reconsider their suitability as a potential partner or even friend.

Looking back, do you think your trust in your partner was blinded by love's emotions? If so, how would you approach a new relationship using what you have learned?

Chances are the only answer to this is yes except in a few rare cases. The answer to the prior question provides guidance for this answer as well.

If you are still married, do you worry about your partner having the patience to "hang in there" while you rebuild trust? How can we help them be patient?

If you are serious about staying with the person then it will be natural for you to worry about this. Easy to say but try not to let this rule you or cause you to live in fear. You are a much stronger person (or will be) because of this and if they do leave, maybe it's the best thing for you in the long run. If they are not able to "hang on" now, what will happen next time there is a crisis? The best thing you can do is encourage them when they are honest. Let them know you appreciate every case of honesty. Also, let them know from time-to-time the progress you believe is being made. If they can see progress then chances are they will be encouraged and not give up.

Chapter 13, Forgiveness as a Part of Recovery

(So, if that is the case,) What would be just compensation to you for your spouse's affair?

This is something only you can determine for yourself. It obviously usually would not include money as in the example. However, if as in my case, your spouse destroyed your finances or even took money from you, you could ask for repayment. You could also ask for a new bank account that only you could control. Otherwise, for some of us it might include many actions such as; providing continuous accountability for where they are, providing phone records and all email accounts and passwords. A heartfelt apology, honesty, slamming the door shut on the lover and couples counseling could all be a part of the "compensation."

In your own circumstances, can you see any benefits to forgiving, even if your partner has left you or refuses to justly compensate you?

This also is one only you can answer. The chapter on forgiveness offers a number of benefits that can come from forgiveness. To help you decide whether, when and how forgiveness might be appropriate, think of the benefits that are most meaningful to you personally.

What might be the adverse consequences of forgiving an unrepentant spouse?

Perhaps there are many but one may simply be that as an unrepentant spouse, they may repeat the behavior and you'll find yourself having to make yet another decision of forgiveness. Another might be that if they continue to be stubborn you will begin to feel that they have also betrayed your act of forgiveness and you may start to regret it. One key to forgiveness is to not force it. Only do it when you feel it is right and that it will help you.

What are the consequences to you of not forgiving?

That can depend on many things. It is possible that you could still carry far too much anger around with you. You also could find yourself under unnecessary stress over a longer period of time. If your religious beliefs strongly urge forgiveness, you could find yourself in a conflict of guilt over feeling you have to versus you want (or don't want) to forgive.

What are the emotional obstacles to forgiveness? How can you personally overcome them?

Some emotional obstacles could be fear that they may use it as a ticket to repeat. Your own anger could continue to get in the way. Hatred for what they did or for them personally could interfere. Feeling that what they did is beyond forgiveness and harboring those feelings for far too long and simple stubbornness can also play a part. One way to overcome these feelings is to identify them and try to rationally think them through. You should decide if they are valid or not and either continue to with-hold your forgiveness or move on with it.

How important is it to you to have your *spouse forgive you* for all the things they told you "forced" them into an affair? Or is that even an issue?

If it is not an issue, you are through with it. If it is, then carefully look to see if there is any real truth to their accusations. Usually there are not but sometimes, there may be issues that you agree may have contributed and just let them know you are sorry and ask for them to forgive you. If you think it over and don't care one way or the other, just drop the issue entirely.

Dear Reader,

Thank you for reading my book.

If you'd like to contact me with feedback, questions related to this book or recovery, I'll be delighted to hear from you. You may email me at firstaid@bellsouth.net or visit my website at: FirstAidforAffairs.com. I wish you complete success and ultimate happiness as you recover.

Richard Alan, June, 2008

ISBN 142510356-1